"García-Johnson is a master of the intersection of decolonial theory and theology. He helps us understand our current moment of 'Babel rebooted' in the authoritarian populist regime of Donald Trump and calls us forward to an exciting vision of 're-existencia' in the Holy Spirit and a church without borders."

—**Robert Chao Romero**
Associate Professor, UCLA

"For those of us on the frontlines of immigrant justice, *Embracing Fear* is both mirror and map. García-Johnson speaks with the clarity of a prophet and the heart of a fellow traveler, showing how fear can become a holy fire that fuels resistance, dignity, and liberation. He dares us to see fear not as failure, but as the birthplace of resistance, justice, and radical hope. This is a guidebook for pastors, organizers, and spiritual seekers who long for a Spirit-led path toward justice, dignity, and communal liberation in the face of empire."

—**Grace Roberts Dyrness**
Community Development Consultant

"When Christianity is colonized by empire, its driving missiology becomes that of perpetuating empire. García-Johnson's book challenges Christians from around the globe to resist empire—manifest as authoritarian populism—by embracing the risk of potential martyrdom that comes with bearing the cross. The result is an ecclesiology rooted in the miracle of Pentecost in which the church is distinguished as a community of compassionate inclusion over against the Babel of a xenophobic monoculture."

—**Rubén Rosario Rodríguez**
Professor of Systematic Theology, Saint Louis University

"In a world increasingly shaped by the politics of fear, populism, necropolitical regimes, and global structures of apartheid, *Embracing Fear* presents a theologically grounded and methodologically provocative response. Drawing on critical theological traditions, Garcia reframes fear not as a condition to be avoided but as a theological locus of agency and moral discernment. Engaging contemporary political realities—from Gaza to immigration, from landlessness to the broader global apartheid order—Oscar García-Johnson challenges readers to resist the passive internalization of fear and instead approach it as a fertile site for pneumatological imagination and prophetic praxis. Urgent and intellectually rigorous, this book contributes meaningfully to current debates in political theology, decolonial theology, and public ethics."

—**Mitri Raheb**
President, Dar al-Kalima University, Bethlehem, Palestine

Embracing Fear

Embracing Fear

—Christian Re-Existence in the Trump Era—

OSCAR GARCÍA-JOHNSON

Foreword by Alexia Salvatierra

CASCADE *Books* • Eugene, Oregon

EMBRACING FEAR
Christian Re-Existence in the Trump Era

Copyright © 2025 Oscar García-Johnson. All rights reserved. Except for brief quotations in critical publications or reviews, no part of this book may be reproduced in any manner without prior written permission from the publisher. Write: Permissions, Wipf and Stock Publishers, 199 W. 8th Ave., Suite 3, Eugene, OR 97401.

Cascade Books
An Imprint of Wipf and Stock Publishers
199 W. 8th Ave., Suite 3
Eugene, OR 97401

www.wipfandstock.com

PAPERBACK ISBN: 979-8-3852-4878-0
HARDCOVER ISBN: 979-8-3852-4879-7
EBOOK ISBN: 979-8-3852-4880-3

Cataloguing-in-Publication data:

Names: García-Johnson, Oscar, author. | Salvatierra Alexia, foreword.

Title: Embracing fear : Christian re-existence in the Trump era / Oscar García Johnson; foreword by Alexia Salvatierra.

Description: Eugene, OR: Cascade Books, 2025 | Includes bibliographical references and index.

Identifiers: ISBN 979-8-3852-4878-0 (paperback) | ISBN 979-8-3852-4879-7 (hardcover) | ISBN 979-8-3852-4880-3 (ebook)

Subjects: LCSH: Fear—Religious aspects—Christianity. | Postcolonial theology. |Public theology. Pentecostalism—global.

Classification: BT83.57 G37 2025 (paperback) | BT83.57 (ebook)

VERSION NUMBER 08/21/25

To the children of Gaza, displaced and grieving,
and to the immigrant children expelled
from the United States—

bound by a shared experience of terror and landlessness.
May your stories haunt our conscience and shape our
re-existence.

Babel is not the last word—Pentecost is.
We scatter therefore we live.

Contents

Foreword by Alexia Salvatierra | ix
Acknowledgments | xiii
Introduction | xv

Chapter 1
Global Apartheid—From Worlds Apart to Apartheid as a World Order | 1

Chapter 2
Choosing the Oppressor—Theopolitical Reflections on the Aftermath of the 2024 US Election | 31

Chapter 3
Political Conformity and the Crisis of Democracy —Authoritarian Populism as the Political and Theological Challenge of Our Time | 56

Chapter 4
From Conforming to Co(i)nspiring—Toward a Post-Abyssal Imagination | 76

Chapter 5
Cracking Babel!—Pentecost Re-Existencia in the Era of Imperial Populism | 100

Epilogue | 121

Bibliography | 137

Foreword

WHEN I THINK ABOUT the core thrust and focus of *Embracing Fear*, two stories come to mind.

One is a personal experience. In 1991, I had the privilege of hearing the (only) Latino General Secretary of the World Council of Churches speak at a small gathering in Northern California. The organization hosting the gathering, Vesper Society, was engaged in supporting President Oscar Arias of Costa Rica in his behind-the-scenes, alternative peace process for El Salvador and Guatemala. President Arias was awarded a Nobel Peace Prize for that successful initiative. At the time when he came to speak, Rev. Dr. Emilio Castro was just finishing up his tenure at the WCC and we were in the final throes of the peace process. The words he spoke are engraved in me; they have come up over and over again during the ensuing years, although, of course, I have no way of knowing whether I remembered them correctly. The gathering was private and his presentation was never published. To the best of my memory, he said, "Over the next twenty years, the world will see increasing political democracy and increasing economic consolidation of power, economic tyranny. The contact between the two will be a schizophrenic experience. People will think of themselves as more free but the they will feel less free. This profound dissonance will create great anxiety. In their anxiety, people will seek simplistic answers and follow demagogues. False religion will obscure this reality and true religion will reveal it."

The other story is not a true story; it's a moment in the film *Bread and Roses*, about Justice for Janitors, the SEIU (Service Employees International Union) campaign that led to a massive victory for low-wage janitors in Los Angeles, attaining living wages, benefits, and a voice in the economic decisions that impact their lives. In the scene, two janitors are on their knees in a hallway of a corporate building and the audience sees legs walk by in business suits carrying briefcases. You can hear their voices speaking as they step over the janitors into the elevator. One janitor turns to the other and says, "Do you know that we have magic powers?" The other one responds, "Us? How so? You are crazy." The first speaker responds, "We have the magic power to become invisible."

This book is about developing a theology and spirituality that makes marginalized and devalued people visible as precious children of God; it is about a process of seeing that starts with exposing the painful inequities that are causing terrible anxiety in our world and then moves to ways to address that anxiety that are both realistic and faithful.

The language of *Embracing Fear* is intentionally dramatic and provocative. In describing deeply rooted inequities, Dr. García-Johnson uses the phrase "global apartheid" and cites Boaventura de Sousa Santos's "abyssal line" as capsule descriptions of the bad news of the exclusion and erasure of millions of the discriminated-against in the current world economic systems and political structures. He ties these descriptions to sweeping historical narratives that also analyze the reasons why these systems and structures are often supported by those who are most wounded and damaged by them.

While Dr. García-Johnson covers a wide range of disciplines in his analysis, ultimately he is most concerned about theology and ministry. He wants to suggest a model for congregational and community resistance that nurtures new life in the midst of death.

Embracing Fear is most compelling when telling the story of the various examples of that new life breaking forth in different places and contexts in our current context. As someone who has been involved in movements all my life, I would place greater stress on the accomplishments of movements over the past fifty years as well as speaking to current realities; I would join Bishop Tutu in affirming that marginalized Christians have been resurrection people in many places and times, not just Friday, Saturday, or even daybreak people. I would also say that some of the theological frameworks used in *Embracing Fear* do not fit my experience on the ground of how hope, love, faith, and joy vanquish paralyzing fear in the marginalized leaders whom I have worked with and shared life with.

However, I deeply value *Embracing Fear*'s provocation to the fresh *sentipensar* (feeling/thinking) of prophetic imagination. In order to be freed from false hope, illusory complacency, and angry despair, every generation needs new language for ancient truths that support action for change. The stories of Spirit-filled rebellion and renewal in *Embracing Fear* are tastes of Pentecost—new approaches to name and embody the way of Jesus for such a time as this that are both recognizable and refreshing. Its innovative structure with thought-provoking questions for community organizers, congregational leaders, and seminary students provides an effective delivery system for the stimulation of our collective creativity. Our current crisis desperately calls for courageous questioning and serious dialogue, rooted in the best gifts of our faith. *Embracing Fear* is designed to take us there; welcome to the journey!

—Rev. Dr. Alexia Salvatierra
Academic Dean, Centro Latino, Fuller Theological Seminary

Acknowledgments

I AM AN IMMIGRANT, a banana republic theologian—made in Jersey City (so I'm told), born in Honduras, and formed in Los Angeles. The moment my mother, C. Margarita Johnson Williams, heard *La Virgencita* say to her, "Leave this land and go to Los Angeles," my *autohistoria* began to take shape. That moment continues to forge meaning—meaning I can only access when I face profound challenges in the present and look both back and ahead. She left USAmerica pregnant with me to save me, and then brought me back to educate me. My first word of gratitude goes to my mom—a fierce and resilient woman who became an immigrant many times over, driven by hopeless economic conditions, political corruption, and social conformity. Her resilience gave me *reexistencia*.

I also thank Karina, Gustavo, and Karla, with whom I embarked on a Celtic ancestry family trip to the UK on the day of the 2024 US presidential election. Our conversations and shared experiences while tracing family migration stories across England, Wales, and Scotland fertilized my imagination, until the seminal ideas that gave birth to this work began to take root.

Embracing Fear would not have come to life as a published text without the strategic assistance of Karen Hamilton Lucas, who served not only as the principal research assistant and style editor but also as one of the peer reviewers for many of the concepts expressed in this book. Her scholarly competence in religious history and political theology was essential. In the same breath, my deep thanks go to Kunăne Hillel, who went above and beyond his role

Acknowledgments

as Instructor in Training (IIT), sticking with the project even after his contract had ended.

I write from my heart, with my mind, and in community. In this spirit, I am especially grateful to the Decolonial Conversation Student Group at Fuller Seminary—led by Greta Bennet, Gregory Conarroe, and Karen H. Lucas—which read and responded to four of the five chapters during the 2024–2025 academic year. I wrote *Embracing Fear* with them as my dialogue partners.

I could not have conceived the concept of "global apartheid" without attending the October 2023 International Conference on "Land, People, and Culture" at Dar al-Kalima University in Bethlehem. Rev. Dr. Mitri Raheb was, simply put, a stellar host. I am not the same after that experience.

Finally, I am deeply indebted to Michael Thomson and Wipf & Stock Publishers, my first publisher, for their steadfast support. I am honored.

Introduction

THIS IS NOT A book I ever planned to write or thought I could—it emerged along the way.

Like the two disciples trudging the Emmaus road in Luke 24, I was walking away from Jerusalem—away from a place that had just shattered my messianic expectations—when the Spirit began piecing this manuscript together. My own Emmaus stretch began on November 5, 2024, the morning a handful of us (all relatives) arrived in London under low, steel-gray clouds. While we chased an unexpected opportunity to trace family roots, news screens at Heathrow scrolled one relentless headline: *TRUMP WINS RETURN TO WHITE HOUSE*. We said almost nothing. Any outcome, we conceded, would bruise someone we loved. What stunned us was not the result itself but the fervor with which many of the very communities targeted by Trump's program—immigrants, former refugees, queer youth, Christian leaders with global missions, the working poor—had carried him back to power.

Thirteen months earlier I had landed at LAX, 7 PM local time, fresh from Bethlehem. Barely twenty-four hours later—exactly fifty years after the 1973 war—the al-Qassam Brigades launched Al-Aqsa Flood, a coordinated surprise that exposed the cracks in Israel's formidable surveillance regime. Influential Palestinian leaders framed the action as an answer to "the ongoing stream of crimes . . . the siege on Gaza, the theft of land for settlements, the denial of refugees' right to return . . . and the seventy-five years of

Zionist occupation," while Israeli and US officials denounced it as Iranian-orchestrated terror designed to derail diplomacy.

I cannot pretend neutrality. Raised "Baptistcostal" in the thick air of dispensationalist Christian Zionism, I was taught to read 1948 as prophetic triumph, and any threat to Israel as treason against God. Yet the land itself kept unmasking my theology. A Hebrew Bible professor first guided me through the 700-plus checkpoints that throttle Palestinian movement; later visits exposed the pageantry of US pilgrims marching West Jerusalem streets in "Donald Trump for President" shirts while Palestinian vendors watched their city renamed by someone else's eschatology.

Those dislocations—London on election night, Gaza at the cusp of war, the US throat-parched in aporophobic panic—braided into a single intuition: fear is the operating system of our age. And so the book you hold, *Embracing Fear: Christian Re-Existence in the Trump Era*, was conceived not as a polemic for political insiders or a treatise for guild theologians, but as a field manual for ordinary disciples learning to breathe—and believe—in an atmosphere saturated with anxiety.

Why *Embracing Fear*?

Throughout these pages I argue that fear, far from being an emotion to be rebuked or medicated, can become fertile ground for Spirit-powered imagination. Authoritarian populism—from Washington to Brasília, from Budapest to Jerusalem—weaponizes dread, promising salvation through sameness: one language, one wall, one flag. It is, as Walter Brueggemann calls it, "fortress mentality"; what Genesis 11 names as Babel's fear of scattering. Contemporary strongmen have merely updated the blueprint with algorithmic surveillance, mass deportation, and competitive authoritarian tactics.

Yet Acts 2 tells another story: dispersion can be the stage for Pentecost. *Embracing Fear* therefore refuses the polite optimism that asks the oppressed to wait for Sunday resurrection while they still bleed through Friday crucifixion. Drawing on "strategic hopelessness" (Miguel De La Torre), I invite readers to inhabit Holy Saturday—not as nihilists, but as co-conspirators who refuse empire's demand for triumphant certainties. Fear, inverted by grace, becomes a generative discipline that pushes communities to shelter immigrants during ICE raids, to host iftar in church basements, to translate worship into the many tongues silenced at Babel.

What the Book Does

Naming the shape of the crisis, chapter 1, "Global Apartheid," traces how coloniality matured into a planetary caste system that assigns some bodies to *Optimus* status and others to disposable *Infimus* categories, policed by what I call the colonial algorithm of humanity. This chapter surveys ten crises every Christian leader now faces—from digital disinformation to ecological collapse—and diagnoses them as symptoms of a single monocultural motherboard.

Exposing fear's political alchemy, chapter 2, "Choosing the Oppressor," unpacks why marginalized voters sometimes ally with leaders who promise their own exclusion. Using historical precedents from British India to Tlaxcala, and contemporary data on Latino/a evangelical support for Trump, I show how authoritarian populism exploits unmet needs and aporophobia (the dread of the poor) to convert victims into defenders of hierarchy.

Mapping the mechanics of political conformity, chapter 3 analyses six social-psychological frameworks—normative influence, social identity, rational choice, cognitive dissonance, structural functionalism, and coercion—to reveal how Christian nationalism provides sacred cover for Babel-logic policies such as voter-ID laws, border militarization, and *Project 2025* deregulation.

Moving from conforming to co-[i]nspiring, chapter 4 argues that resistance must cross the "abyssal line" Boaventura de Sousa Santos describes—those epistemic trenches separating human from nonhuman, citizen from illegal. Here I sketch practices of

Introduction

intercultural translation and covenantal solidarity that transform manufactured fear into transnational hope.

Envisioning Pentecost *Re-Existir*, chapter 5 imagines the church as a pluriversal "assemblage" of Spirit-activated communities—Zapatista *caracoles* in Chiapas, Kichwa guardians of Ecuador's *selva viviente*, migrant sanctuaries in US parking lots—living prototypes of a kingdom Babel could never engineer.

For Whom Is This Book?

A student exposed to this material recently wrote, "This book gave words to the horrid reality of today and how to work toward a different future." She is exactly my target reader: someone living at the crossroads of discipleship and disorientation who refuses to outsource moral agency to politicians or pundits. While public theologians, ethicists, and social scientists will recognize the footnotes, *Embracing Fear* is crafted for:

- *Grassroots organizers* seeking theological grammar for street-level justice work.
- *Pastors and lay leaders* wrestling with congregational polarization and Christian-Zionist triumphalism and antisemitism, Islamophobia, and Latinoaphobia.
- *Undergraduate and seminary classes* studying decolonial praxis, political theology, or Indigenous hermeneutics—each chapter ends with discussion questions for the classroom, the church, and the picket line.
- *Spirit-haunted skeptics* who love Jesus's prophetic praxis but distrust the religion welded to imperial nostalgia.

How the Journey Began

London's clouds, Bethlehem's checkpoints, and a US ballot box streaked with Christian dominionism converged in one visceral

Introduction

image: Sobhi Qouta's painting *Gaza*. A tall gray wall slices heaven; a figure named Homeros strums his "immortal melody . . . wounds of consecutive calamities . . . passion, tears, spirit." That visual melody lodged in my gut when I first saw it at Dar al-Kalima University, Bethlehem, in 2023. It sounded like my own inherited theology cracking under history's weight, like the hush of churches that decried Nazism too late and now mute themselves before settler violence, like the silence of immigrant congregations paralyzed by the threat of deportation.

I began writing in trains between Edinburgh and King's Cross, sketching links between West Bank sieges and ICE detentions, between South African apartheid and "illegal alien" rhetoric, between Brexit isolationism and the algorithmic policing of truth. I wrote as one haunted by fear but unwilling to worship at its golden tower.

What I Hope You Hear

By the final page, I pray you will embrace fear—not the fake fear peddled by demagogues, but the *holy terror* that sends Mary to sing of toppled thrones and Isaiah to announce good news to the poor. Such fear is the doorway to re-existence—the Spirit-drenched decision to live otherwise, scatter boldly, and improvise Pentecost wherever Babel builds another wall.

If you are weary of Babel's single-tongue liturgies, welcome. If you have tasted the "ferocious disregard for the pain of others" that Fanon named, take courage. The chapters ahead do not offer cheap reassurance. They offer something sturdier: a theology forged in Gaza's shadow and London's drizzle, tempered by the votes of neighbors who fear you, yet animated by an *Espíritu* already dancing in occupied zip codes.

Let us step onto the Emmaus road together. We may discover, in the breaking of fearful bread, that Christ has been walking beside us all along—whispering, *Do not be afraid of fear; turn and face it, for I have overcome the world.*

Chapter 1

Global Apartheid
—From Worlds Apart to Apartheid as a World Order—

"Pain shudders through the arteries of global society. Day after day passes by as the genocide against the Palestinian people continues and the conflicts in the Great Lakes region of Africa and Sudan escalate. More and more people slip into absolute poverty as arms companies' profits soar. These realities have hardened society, allowing people to bury their heads and ignore the horrors unfolding across the world. Ferocious disregard for the pain of others has become a way to protect oneself from the inflation of suffering."[1]
—*Dareen Tatour*

OURS IS A TIME that calls for careful listening, strategic apprehension, and courageous action. The world speaks to us in dissonant but urgent ways—echoes of trauma, inequity, and resilience from the past, present, and future. These messages form a collective plea for survival and life otherwise. Yet the siren sounds of urgency are often muted by distortions rooted in disproportionate power and

---

1. Cited in Prashad, "Resist, My People, Resist."

privilege leading to a "ferocious disregard for the pain of others." As Frantz Fanon observed in *The Wretched of the Earth*, the marginalized and disenfranchised—the "wretched"—bear the brunt of systemic mismanagement by global systems of inequality and domination.[2]

Today, we face the unraveling of a world order where life itself is imperiled by the intertwining forces of privatized Christian morality and the systemic normalization of inequality, structural violence, and environmental collapse. This world order—the Western global order—traces its origins to the colonial enterprises that laid the foundation for modern nation-states. Over time, these colonial structures have evolved and consolidated into the current configuration of liberal democracies and so-called "free" market economies. At its core, this system perpetuates power imbalances and privileges certain identities, geographies, and economic frameworks, while naturalizing the exploitation of marginalized populations and the environment. The consequences of this historical trajectory are manifest in the growing crises of social inequity, global unrest, and ecological devastation—outcomes that expose the fragility and unsustainability of this decaying order.[3]

We will explore how, at the heart of these crises, lies a modern form of global apartheid—a structure of systemic separation, hierarchy, and exclusion that divides humanity into categories of privilege and disposability. Global apartheid functions through political, economic, and cultural systems, reinforced by ideological

---

2. Fanon, *Wretched of the Earth*.

3. I acknowledge that the phrase "a world in decay" may carry a negative connotation, suggesting an absence of human advances, which is not my intent. I reject totalizing or triumphalist discourses rooted in the rhetoric of modernity, progress, and civilizing democracy. While global advancements in health, education, and connectivity are undeniable, they coexist with significant challenges such as ecological degradation, mental health crises, and rising inequality. Progress remains uneven, deeply context-dependent, and influenced by positionality, shaping either optimistic or critical perspectives. My view aligns with the *Epistemologies of the South*, particularly Boaventura de Sousa Santos's concept of the "abyssal line," which highlights colonial, capitalist, and patriarchal systems that render the oppressed invisible, irrelevant, and non-existent (*End of Cognitive Empire*).

(often religious) beliefs that perpetuate divisions between the powerful and the powerless, the included and the excluded.

Ten Global Crises of Our Time for Christian Leaders

In the fall of 2024, during a lecture on "The Ten Global Challenges of Our Time for Christian Leaders" delivered to evangelical leaders of the Global South, I witnessed their shock at how deeply these challenges resonated across their diverse cultural and geographical contexts. I presented the following challenges:

1. *Political Polarization*—How do political entanglements distort the meaning of the gospel, and how can we navigate faith in a divided world?
2. *Generational Differences*—How can we bridge generational gaps while fostering unity in the church?
3. *Justice and Reconciliation*—How do we confront systemic racism, inequity, corruption, and ecological destruction while building a just and reconciled world?
4. *Sexual Scandals and Sexual Diversity*—How can we balance responsible views on sexuality with compassionate morality?
5. *Doctrinal Divisions*—How do we interpret Scripture differently yet faithfully, centering Christopraxis as our shared hermeneutic?
6. *Cultural Competence vs. Traditional Faithfulness*—How can we engage cultural contexts as a church without defaulting to a monocultural orthodoxy?
7. *Decline in Church Attendance and Rising Unbelief*—How do we walk alongside nonbelievers and ex-believers outside institutional church structures?
8. *Gender Inclusion in Leadership*—How can women's perspectives reshape church leadership and renew the church's impact in the world?

9. *Prosperity Gospel vs. Global Poverty*—How can we challenge wealth-centered ministries and inspire solidarity with the poor?

10. *Digital Revolution and AI Theology*—How can we critically embrace digital and AI technologies while cultivating authentic community in diverse cultural contexts?

After I presented these challenges, a pressing question arose: how is it possible that these issues feel universally urgent, despite our diverse locations, traditions, and vocations? My response was simple: we have been conformed to a monocultural, metropolitan, global Christian model of citizenship—a global design operated through an epistemic mechanism known by decolonial critics as the *Colonial Matrix of Power (CMP)*. This cognitive and geopolitical mechanism generates the problems and offers the solutions to the very challenges we discussed.

Ironically, in the original context of Western political thought and religion, virtue in the service of the community was considered foundational to political life. It played a less instrumental and individualistic role than it does in modern colonial times. However, the modern rhetoric of the separation of church and state, reflecting the misconception that faith and reason have distinct and separate domains, reduced religion to a utilitarian and individualistic function. This shift contrasts sharply with its early origins, where faith and reason were often experienced in critical dialogue —even to the point of challenging each other while coexisting for the collective good.[4]

If my argument on the role of reason and faith for the collective good in ancient political life is true, which I think it is, then the transformation from ancient to modern political thought had profound and often devastating consequences, both for Europe's

---

4. Two philosophical works referenced on this matter are Farrer, *Faith and Speculation*, and Frank, *Philosophical Understanding and Religious Truth*. Both Farrer and Frank emphasize the integral relationship between faith and reason in classical and early Christian thought, critiquing modern separations and individualistic reductions of religion as distortions of its original communal and holistic purpose.

fragmented and tribal societies and for populations worldwide who became subjugated under colonial rule. Ancient political thought, rooted in the integration of reason and faith, prioritized communal well-being and a teleological understanding of human and societal purpose. The shift to modernity, marked by the dominance of rationalism and individualism, fragmented these cohesive structures, eroding the moral and ethical frameworks that had sustained collective life.

In Europe, this transformation exacerbated divisions, leading to the weakening of traditional communities and the rise of competitive, self-interested states. Globally, modernity became a tool for justifying colonial domination, as the universalizing claims of modern political and economic thought marginalized non-European systems and subjugated their populations under exploitative colonial orders. This critique aligns with the philosophical frameworks of Enrique Dussel, who underscores modernity's colonial underpinnings, and Alasdair MacIntyre, who highlights the loss of communal and virtue-based ethics in modernity. Their work invites a reevaluation of this transition, emphasizing the need to recover ethical systems rooted in solidarity, liberation, and the common good.[5] This catastrophic shift became visible after 1492, with the *Doctrine of Discovery*, which provided the ideological and theological justification for colonial expansion and domination.

Let us now examine some of the most foundational conceptions of political thought and the role of religion in the early development of Western geopolitics. Following this, we will address the catastrophic epistemological and geopolitical shifts introduced by colonial modernity.

Ancient Roots of Western Political Thought and the Role of Religion

Religion has been integral to the philosophical and political thought of pre-Socratic and post-Socratic Graeco-Roman settings,

---

5. See Dussel, *Ethics of Liberation*, and MacIntyre, *After Virtue*.

influencing political structures through practices such as the integration of religious rituals into civic ceremonies and the use of divine authority to legitimize rulers.[6] For instance, city-states like Athens incorporated public worship of deities such as Athena into their political life, while Roman emperors often claimed divine favor to bolster their authority.[7] In Homeric epics, the gods were depicted as active agents who controlled natural phenomena and human fortunes, necessitating worship and sacrifices to appease their desires.[8] This theological worldview set the stage for philosophical critiques and re-evaluations, particularly in the works of Plato, who sought to redefine the role of religion in public life.[9]

Plato argued for a political role for religion while critiquing the prevailing conceptions of the gods and the uses of religious practice. For Plato, true religion was closely aligned with philosophy—the love of wisdom and the pursuit of truth and the good life. This alignment influenced his views on governance, as he argued that rulers should embody philosophical virtues to create just laws and harmonious societies.[10]

Plato's concept of philosopher-kings in *The Republic* exemplifies this, as he envisioned leaders guided by reason and a commitment to the common good, ensuring that governance reflected the pursuit of higher truths.[11] Through the Socratic method, Plato explored the cultivation of a virtuous life reflective of higher ideals: the Good, the True, and the Beautiful.[12] Religion, in this philosophical framework, was valuable insofar as it contributed to the production of virtuous individuals who could establish communities (poleis) and laws aligned with natural order, ultimate truth,

6. Price, *Rituals and Power*, 110–15.

7. See Burkert, *Greek Religion*, and Zaidman and Pantel, *Religion in the Ancient Greek City*, 35–40.

8. See for instance Homer, *Iliad*, 23; Homer, *Odyssey*, 275.

9. Gill, "Plato on True and False Religion."

10. Allen, *Plato's 'Republic,'* 85–90.

11. Plato, *Republic*, 196–205.

12. See for instance, Plato, "Allegory of the Sun" in *Republic*, 196–205. See also Annas, *Introduction to Plato's Republic*, 145–50.

and the ultimate Good.[13] This vision placed religion and philosophy in service of communal well-being and justice.[14]

Public Leadership and Justice

This philosophical framework finds resonance in Cicero's writings, particularly his vision of justice in governance.[15] In *De Officiis* (1.25), Cicero asserts that leaders should act as guardians (*tutelae*) of the state, prioritizing the well-being of their fellow citizens over personal interests.[16] He echoes Plato's precept that rulers must care for the whole body politic, ensuring their administration serves the public good rather than private gain. This conception of leadership reflects an ethical framework that aligns political service with virtue and the pursuit of the common good.[17]

Cicero's analogy of the state as a *tutela* underscores the leader's responsibility to uphold justice as the highest guiding principle.[18] Justice, in this sense, is not merely adherence to laws but an active commitment to the welfare of the entire community. Cicero illustrates this principle in *De Officiis* by emphasizing the moral obligation of rulers to prioritize the common good over private interest, such as when he argues that public funds should be managed with integrity to serve the broader citizenry rather than personal gain. By situating the role of the ruler within a moral and philosophical framework, Cicero encapsulates the core principles of ancient political thought: service, justice, and the prioritization of the common good.[19]

---

13. Annas, *Introduction to Plato's Republic*, 125–30; Zuckert, *Plato's Philosophers*, 300–305.
14. Voegelin, *Plato and Aristotle*, 130–35.
15. See Everitt, *Cicero*, 210–15; Mitchell, *Cicero*, 145–50.
16. Cicero, *Officiis*, 1.25.
17. Harrington, *Commonwealth of Oceana*, 60–65. Harrington links Cicero's concept of *tutela* to later philosophies on public service and justice.
18. Atkins, *Cicero on Politics*, 95–100.
19. Zetzel, *Cicero and the Late Roman Republic*, 115–20.

Contrasts with Modern Political Thought

The ethical and philosophical foundations of ancient Western political thought highlight a stark contrast with modern Western geopolitics.[20] A basic Socratic premise—that "He who wrongs another person always damages his own happiness more than his victim's"—permeates ancient Greek political thought, influences early Christian doctrine, and becomes a cornerstone of later Western ethical traditions.[21] This principle underscores the interconnectedness of personal virtue and communal well-being.

As we have shown, Plato's *Republic* presents a foundational vision for Western politics centered around philosopher-kings—rulers governed by reason, virtue, and an unyielding commitment to the common good. In contrast, modern politics, in contemporary cases driven by populism, factionalism, and self-interest, deviates significantly from this ideal.[22] Cicero, following Plato's political philosophy, emphasized natural law and the importance of a virtuous ruling class committed to justice and the welfare of the entire community. Contemporary nation-states, however, often witness the erosion of shared ethical foundations, where governance prioritizes short-term political gain over enduring principles of justice.

With some hesitation, I would suggest that even Niccolò Machiavelli, in *The Prince*, acknowledged the harsh realities of power, emphasizing the necessity of pragmatism and, at times, ruthless decision-making in governance. However, he also critiqued politics that failed to achieve even pragmatic objectives such as stability and the public good, instead becoming entangled in dysfunction and self-serving agendas.[23]

---

20. Voegelin, *Order and History*, vol. III, 90–95.

21. Vlantos, *Socrates, Ironist and Moral Philosopher*, 5.

22. Barber, *Strong Democracy*, 120–25.

23. Machiavelli, *Prince*, 98–103. See also McCormick's perspective on Machiavelli's critique of rulers who fail to achieve stability by acting for personal gain rather than for public welfare in *Machiavellian Democracy*, 75–80.

Jean-Jacques Rousseau's *The Social Contract* proposed a vision of governance guided by the general will, ensuring the coexistence of collective good and individual freedom.[24] However, in today's modern states, the general will is often subverted by economic inequality and corporate interests. For example, the disproportionate influence of lobbying in the United States illustrates how the priorities of powerful entities can override the broader public interest, undermining Rousseau's ideal of governance for the collective good. Modern states, marked by economic inequality, corporate dominance, and civic disengagement, often subvert the general will Rousseau idealized.[25] This alienation of citizens from political processes underscores the need to revisit foundational principles of justice, virtue, and the common good articulated in ancient thought.

From Ancient Political Philosophy to Modern Colonial Politics

In tracing the evolution of Western political thought from ancient philosophy and theology to modern colonial politics, we can advance three key arguments.

Virtue as Foundational to Political Life in Western Thought

Historically, classical political and religious traditions, as we have shown, placed virtue at the core of public life. Classical thinkers like Aristotle and Plato, alongside Christian theologians such as Augustine and Aquinas, regarded virtue as essential to the well-being of the *polis* (city-state) or community. Aristotle, for example, conceived politics as an extension of ethics, aiming to cultivate virtuous citizens who contribute to the common good. Early

---

24. Rousseau, *Social Contract*, 62–65.

25. Rousseau, *Social Contract*, 112–15. Also see Williams, *Rousseau's Social Contract*, 180–85, as this source discusses the tension between Rousseau's ideals and modern corporate and political realities.

Christian thought similarly emphasized virtues like charity and justice as central to fostering harmonious, God-fearing communities, underscoring the collective dimension of moral responsibility.

The Colonial Shift: Instrumental and Individualistic Roles of Virtue

The transition from antiquity to colonial modernity marked a significant transformation in the role and perception of virtue. Colonial administrations often prioritized personal piety and morality over communal obligations, using missionary efforts to instill obedience rather than fostering collective welfare. Bartolomé de Las Casas's *A Brief Account of the Destruction of the Indies* (1542) illustrates how virtue was co-opted to justify exploitation, rather than serving the collective good. The introduction of private property laws and the rise of Enlightenment individualism reframed virtue as adherence to personal economic productivity, distancing it from its communal roots. Additionally, colonial powers frequently deployed religious and moral rhetoric for utilitarian purposes, enabling economic exploitation and cultural domination under the guise of virtue.

The Rhetoric of Church-State Separation and the Individualization of Religion

The Enlightenment's emphasis on the separation of church and state, as articulated by thinkers like Locke and Jefferson, contributed to the privatization of religion. In efforts to protect individual freedoms and prevent sectarian conflict, religion was increasingly viewed as a personal choice rather than a communal force. This shift, enshrined in constitutions like that of the United States, reduced religion to a largely individualistic and utilitarian role, further weakening its connection to collective responsibilities and the common good. The reframing of religion as a private matter dovetails with the broader Enlightenment trend toward individualism, underscoring how these developments diverged from ancient and early Christian conceptions of virtue and governance.

1492: From Classical Rationalism to Instrumental Coloniality

From the perspective of the Global South, what is often missing in philosophical critiques of modernity is the unacknowledged internal logic of modernity—namely, coloniality. To illustrate this, a brief philosophical comparison is instructive. Prominent Western philosophers such as Leo Strauss and Alasdair MacIntyre critique modernity for its departure from classical rationalism and its diminished emphasis on virtue as foundational to the collective good. They contend that natural law and virtue were transformed, leading to individualism, fragmentation, and incoherence, ultimately culminating in relativism.[26]

In contrast, notable philosophers and epistemologists from the Global South, including Enrique Dussel and Boaventura de Sousa Santos, extend this critique beyond modernity to classical rationalism and virtue itself, pointing out their Hellenocentric biases and universalist pretensions.[27] While Dussel and de Sousa Santos share the critique of modernity's instrumental reason, they also foreground the logic of coloniality, highlighting how colonial systems appropriated rationalism and virtue as tools for domination and exploitation. This critical perspective invites a deeper interrogation.

In *Discourse on Inequality: On the Origin and Basis of Inequality Among Men* (1755), Rousseau reflects: "The first man who, having enclosed a piece of ground, bethought himself of saying 'This is mine,' and found people simple enough to believe him, was the real founder of civil society."[28] Although Rousseau did

---

26. See Strauss, *Natural Right and History*, 120–25; MacIntyre, *After Virtue*, 150–55.

27. See Dussel, *Ethics of Liberation*, 250–55; Santos, *Epistemologies of the South*, 100–105.

28. Rousseau, *Discourse on Inequality*, 63.

not directly address the immorality of the European invasion and occupation of Abya Yala (the so-called "New World"), his critique of the privatization of land and territory in his context is arguably informed by the known consequences of European conquests. These consequences—genocide, ethnocide, and ecocide—were well-documented in Europe during his time, albeit without the depth of connotation these terms evoke today.[29]

The cognitive and instrumental shift in Western political thought did not occur in a vacuum, nor did it emerge solely within Europe. It developed in liminal spaces—at the intersection of cultures—through oppressive and asymmetrical exchanges between European powers and the native civilizations of Abya Yala, as well as those of Africa and Asia. A critical turning point was the Ottoman Empire's control of trade routes, which constrained European economic growth. The search for alternative trade routes became imperative, leading to expeditions funded by the Iberian crown. These explorers, heading westward, inadvertently encountered the Atlantic and "discovered" themselves in the territories of Ayiti (later named Hispaniola).

In other words, this cartographic accident—rooted in real events, spaces, and encounters—transformed European political traditions and theological visions of society. It gave rise to a powerful cognitive mechanism capable of reimagining materiality, symbols, and human aspirations into unprecedented world designs. Europe's social imaginary was profoundly reshaped as it encountered the vastness and diversity of Anáhuac (Mesoamerica), Tahuantinsuyu (South America), and Ayiti (the Caribbean).

The epistemic transformations of the sixteenth century, catalyzed by the so-called "discovery" of the New World, allowed a handful of Western powers to reimagine themselves as global

---

29. The legality of the conquest of the "West Indies" and the assertion of territorial "rights" were subjects of intense debate among legal theologians in the sixteenth and seventeenth centuries, including John Mair (Scotland), Ginés de Sepúlveda, Francisco de Vitoria, and Bartolomé de Las Casas (Spain). These debates highlight the philosophical significance attributed to land occupation and demonstrate how an epistemic shift was already underway, theologically framing a geopolitics that would later underpin colonial projects.

landlords while relegating Indigenous civilizations to labor forces and landlessness. These transformations redefined Western political philosophies and theologies concerning land, international law, labor, culture, urban development, and plural coexistence, embedding coloniality at the heart of modernity.

Today's global migration, occupations, and apartheids—including land occupation, settler colonialism, forced migration, exile, massive deportation, and hyper-emphasis on border protection for national security and prosperity—represent a five-hundred-year problem. These crises are directly tied to global designs built with immense political and economic imagination and legitimized by Westernizing theologies of the land. The so-called discovery of the Atlantic route and the "encounter" with a New World of wealth was, in essence, a cartographic accident that initiated these developments. It is within this historical and philosophical context that we can understand why intellectuals, Western and non-Western, schooled in the "master's narratives," have become the most compelling critics of Western politics, democracy, and cognitive progress. Such is the case with thinkers like John Stuart Mill, Hannah Arendt, and Frantz Fanon.

John Stuart Mill, in *On Liberty* (1859), championed pluralism, individual liberty, and the protection of minoritized rights as core principles of just governance. He critiqued majoritarian politics, cultural homogenization, and systemic inequalities for undermining pluralism and liberty. Hannah Arendt, in *The Origins of Totalitarianism* (1951) and *The Human Condition* (1958), critiqued the rise of bureaucratic and technocratic governance. She argued that these structures alienate citizens and prioritize administrative efficiency over democratic engagement and justice. Arendt highlighted how modern nation-states, in their obsession with order and control, often disregard the rich pluralism and active citizenship that define a vibrant and just society. Frantz Fanon, in *The Wretched of the Earth*, examined how colonial legacies and systemic inequalities shaped modern nation-states into tools of oppression rather than liberation. Fanon exposed how modern governance perpetuates historical injustices, failing to achieve the equitable and pluralistic society envisioned by earlier thinkers.

These critiques converge on the idea that modern states, despite their rhetoric of progress (what Walter Mignolo refers to as modernity's rhetoric), often undermine the very ideals they claim to uphold. More precisely, contemporary states, shaped by neoliberalism and profit-driven interpretations of Marxism, tend to fulfill these principles selectively, privileging a particular class of individuals—those we might term "Optimus." This sets the stage for the argument in the next section, where we will examine global monoculturalism as the foundation of what we call Global Apartheid.

Global Monoculturalism and the Colonial Matrix of Power

The most challenging critique to modern nation-state ideology, right or left, is emerging from the margins and borders of social sciences, literary theory, political thought, and liberation theologies. Decoloniality or the Decolonial Option, as it is usually referred to, is a multi-world and multi-epistemological conversation informing grassroots movements, Western and non-Western academia, and public intellectuals in the hope of decentering whiteness, Westernization, neoliberalism, patriarchy, and religious fundamentalism. One of the most significant contributions of this intellectual and grassroots movement is the attempt to explain why, as we have illustrated at the beginning in this chapter, the oppressed and the oppressor can continue to coexist around the world without a significant change in the equation of global structural injustice and oppression.

The so-called Colonial Matrix of Power (Aníbal Quijano, Walter Mignolo) can be described as a regenerative model of thinking, being, and acting in the world. It presupposes that the European conquest and invention of the "New World" constituted a foundational creation narrative later replicated in colonial projects worldwide. The establishment of the colonial order in the Americas—a multi-world and intercontinental geopolitics—and the emergence of Western modernity across continents represent two sides of the same coin. Consequently, colonial modernity transcends a single historical period known as colonialism, evolving into a new symbolic and material way of life in the modern world.

The Colonial Matrix of Power, through colonial modernity, encompasses multiple domains such as economy, geography—including life and ecological spaces—the valuation and concept of humanity (*humanitas*), authority, and subjectivities. This five-centuries-old model of global design operates as a colonial algorithm, reproducing identities, loyalties, and privileges through global circuits.

The Framework of Monocultural Christianity: A Critical Analysis

Elsewhere I have elaborated on global monoculturalism as follows:

> Monoculturalism functions as a [colonial algorithmic] mode of framing human value and designing global power and privilege. It is not about one individual or country or empire. It's more ubiquitous. Likened to the motherboard of the most powerful supercomputer formatted by an equally powerful software, monoculturalism produces codes in the public, private, and religious [operating] systems resulting in global designs embedded in real life. Except this type of global technology (monoculturalism) has been operating and being perfected for five hundred years, at least. Integrated in the monocultural logic board, we find patriarchy, monologue, monopoly, and monotopia. I am suggesting here that such a powerful global design system in the West produces prototypes (in the center and the peripheries) in the form of structures conforming to the modern idea of civility, progress, and order—and hidden within is coloniality. In other words, the traditional Western establishment follows this modern/colonial prototype.[30]

30. García-Johnson, *Spirit Outside the Gate*, 270–71.

When applied to Christianity, monocultural Christianity operates as a global framework of dominance, organizing societal power, privilege, and human value through a sophisticated system rooted in biblical-theological language and the Colonial Matrix of Power (CMP). This system merges symbolic and material structures to shape spaces where exemplary humanity (termed *Optimus*) is celebrated, while others deemed subhuman (*Infimus*) are rendered disposable.

Central to this framework is a sophisticated *colonial algorithm of human hierarchies,* which categorizes and ranks individuals based on fourteen criteria: male, white, North Atlantic, learned, cisgender, married, fertile, Western Christian, traditional,[31] capitalist, able-bodied, adult, productive, and documented. This algorithm, paired with normalization processes, sustains Monocultural Christianity's dominance through four interrelated mechanisms: Cultural Supremacy, Intellectual Imperialism, Institutional Rule, and Political Conformity. Together, these components configure a world where power is centralized and exclusion institutionalized.

Cultural Supremacy: The Ideological Bedrock

Cultural supremacy establishes the ideological foundation of Monocultural Christianity by elevating specific identities, values, and practices above all others. The algorithm's ideal traits—such as male, white, cisgender, and North Atlantic—define the framework for "exemplary" humanity. These norms are legitimized through patriarchal authority, which sustains male white dominance in governance, economics, and social life. Cultural narratives function as monologues, silencing alternative perspectives and ensuring the dominant worldview is perpetuated without question. Governance operates as a monopoly, creating a system where only those who fit within the algorithm's parameters are valued

---

31. This category applies to the two predominant political traditions in the West—particularly in the United States: liberalism and conservatism. One can be traditionally progressive or conservative and still benefit from the privileges produced by the algorithm.

or included. At the heart of this system lies the vision of a "monotopia," a homogenized utopia that celebrates uniformity and erases diversity. Cultural supremacy thus sustains the symbolic and material spaces where the logic of *Optimus* and *Infimus* flourishes, solidifying hierarchies and marginalizing dissent.

Intellectual Imperialism: Knowledge as Control

The framework of Monocultural Christianity relies heavily on Intellectual Imperialism to control systems of knowledge and meaning. This mechanism prioritizes Eurocentric, Western Christian epistemologies while dismissing alternative intellectual traditions, such as Indigenous, non-Western, and subaltern ways of knowing. This intellectual dominance enforces the algorithm's hierarchical categories, ensuring that only the traits associated with *Optimus* (e.g., learned, adult, cisgender, "able," etc.) are reflected in educational, theological, and cultural institutions. By merging biblical-theological language with the logic of the CMP, intellectual imperialism erases knowledge systems that challenge the hierarchical order. This epistemic monopoly ensures that Monocultural Christianity remains unchallenged, perpetuating a narrow, exclusionary worldview where exemplary humanity is defined by rigid and exclusionary traits.

Institutional Rule: Systemic Enforcement

Institutions such as governments, schools, and religious organizations are the structural enforcers of Monocultural Christianity. Through Institutional Rule, the algorithm's traits are embedded into the functioning of societal systems, creating material and symbolic spaces where inclusion is contingent on conformity. For example, individuals who are not productive, documented, or capitalist-aligned are systematically excluded from accessing institutional power and resources. Institutions act as gatekeepers, ensuring that power and privilege are concentrated among those who meet the algorithm's criteria. By operationalizing the normalization processes of patriarchal authority and monopolistic governance, institutional rule creates durable systems of exclusion that perpetuate the marginalization of those labeled as *Infimus*.

Political Conformity: The Enforcement Arm

Finally, Political Conformity enforces the framework by requiring alignment with the colonial algorithm's checklist for social and political inclusion. Traits such as Western Christian, traditional, capitalist, and fertile are politically idealized, shaping policies and social norms that marginalize individuals who deviate from these traits (e.g., poor immigrants, Muslims, queer individuals, etc.). Those who fail to meet these standards—whether due to gender, race, religion, or socioeconomic status—are excluded from political representation and denied access to societal benefits. Political conformity ensures the system's survival by aligning governance and policy with the algorithm's values, reinforcing the divide between *Optimus* and *Infimus* and ensuring that dissent is suppressed (through national security policies).

A Dialectical System of Domination

Monocultural Christianity thrives on a dialectic between its internal normalization processes and the external categories defined by the colonial algorithm of human hierarchies. The processes of patriarchal authority, monopolistic governance, single narratives, and exclusionary visions create the symbolic and material conditions for the algorithm to function. Simultaneously, the algorithm's fourteen categories—male, white, North Atlantic, and so on—shape how power and privilege are distributed in society. This dialectical relationship ensures that exemplary humanity is continually celebrated, while others are systematically subhumanized and excluded.

Overall, then, Monocultural Christianity operates as a global system of domination, legitimizing power and privilege through its sophisticated colonial algorithm and normalization processes. Cultural supremacy establishes the ideological foundation, intellectual imperialism enforces epistemic control, institutional rule embeds exclusion into systemic structures, and political conformity ensures compliance. By merging theological and colonial logics, this framework perpetuates a rigid hierarchy that marginalizes diversity and sustains inequality. To dismantle this system, it is crucial to confront its foundations, disrupt its mechanisms, and advocate for new paradigms that prioritize equity, inclusion, and the multiplicity of human experience.

In summary, the schematic critique outlined above illustrates how monoculturalism as a framework of being in the world, illustrated through monocultural Christianity, actively participates in and reconstitutes the Colonial Matrix of Power by sustaining a restrictive framework that marginalizes individuals and communities misaligned with its values. By normalizing patriarchal authority, political conformity, and intellectual exclusivity, this system perpetuates entrenched structures of inequality. The processes of normalization—patriarchal authority, monopolistic governance, and exclusionary visions—work to maintain a singular, hegemonic worldview. This analysis challenges readers to critically examine the societal norms and institutions that uphold monocultural dominance and to advocate for inclusive frameworks that celebrate and embrace diversity. Collectively, these cumulative colonial operations manifest as a global apartheid, shaping the contours of contemporary power and exclusion.

A Fractured World: Global Apartheid in the Making

At the heart of today's global crises lies a modern form of apartheid—a structure of systemic separation, hierarchy, and exclusion that divides humanity into categories of privilege and disposability. Global apartheid operates through interconnected systems of power: political, economic, cultural, and ideological. It mirrors the racialized apartheid policies of South Africa, extending their logic to global structures that privilege some populations while marginalizing others.

The term *apartheid*, meaning "separateness" in Afrikaans, refers to the institutionalized system of racial segregation and economic exclusion imposed in South Africa (1948–1994). Under apartheid:

- The white minority enjoyed political dominance, economic privilege, and land ownership.
- The Black majority and other racialized groups were relegated to inferior citizenship, forced into segregated homelands, and denied access to resources.

Apartheid was justified through colonial logic: Black South Africans were cast as inferior and incapable of managing the nation's resources. As Nelson Mandela argued, apartheid was a crime against humanity, sustained by violence, exploitation, and fear.

Modern-day Palestine presents a striking parallel to South African apartheid. Scholars such as Ilan Pappé and Mitri Raheb provide in-depth analyses of the colonial structures sustaining Israel's treatment of Palestinians. Pappé's *The Ethnic Cleansing of Palestine* (2009) documents the systematic displacement of Palestinians in 1948, when Zionist forces expelled over 700,000 people from their homes. This event, known as the Nakba, marked the beginning of a state-led project of ethnic cleansing. Key features of this regime include:

- *Spatial Segregation*: Palestinians are confined to fragmented territories resembling South Africa's Bantustans. The West Bank's division by Israeli settlements and military checkpoints mirrors apartheid's logic of spatial control.
- *Economic Exclusion*: As Mitri Raheb argues in *Decolonizing Palestine* (2020), economic policies restrict Palestinian development. Raheb describes how dependency on Israeli markets, restrictions on movement, and land confiscations stifle Palestinian economic sovereignty.

- *Legal Discrimination*: Israel's legal system privileges Jewish citizens while marginalizing Palestinians. Laws such as the Nation-State Law institutionalize this inequality, codifying Palestinians' second-class status.

- *Violence and Displacement*: Pappé's work highlights ongoing military aggression and forced evictions, perpetuating a cycle of displacement and dispossession.

These policies have been labeled apartheid by prominent human rights organizations, including Amnesty International (2022) and Human Rights Watch (2021). Raheb's analysis underscores the need to view Palestine through a decolonial lens, challenging the narratives that sustain global indifference to Palestinian suffering.

Apartheid as a World Order

The likelihood of a world order emerging on a global stage of apartheid—with its moral character, structural constitution, and legal imagination of citizenship and property ownership—might once have been dismissed as a cynical critique of global democracy, espoused by those who have much to challenge in the status quo and little to lose during moments of historical rupture. However, I believe this is no longer the case. I align with Walter Mignolo's assertion that, in the aftermath of the 2001 "9/11" attacks in the United States and the devastating, unfounded retaliation by the US against Iraq in the Middle East, "In the last few decades, no global-political, epistemic, or aesthetic phenomenon can be explained without the concept of coloniality."[32]

A world health and status crisis imposed by the unexpected 2019 global pandemic along with the solidification of informational capitalism and militarism and the reconstitution of global politics due to Brexit and the new US populist era of Donald Trump have only strengthened Mignolo's view of world orders and geopolitical designs.

32. Mignolo, "Decolonizing Western Epistemology/Building Decolonial Epistemology," 20.

Today's Geopolitical Framing: "Global US [Israel]" and "Global Illegal Aliens [Palestine]"

The transition from global coloniality to global apartheid is starkly illustrated through the US-Israel relationship, a partnership that operates not only as a geopolitical alliance but also as a deeply symbolic hypostasis of global power dynamics. This relationship, as Mitri Raheb and others have argued, is fundamentally triangulated by ultra-right Judeo-Christian ideologies, the misuses of the Bible, and the material realities of land and power.[33] Together, these elements form the ideological backbone of a global apartheid system that enforces hierarchies of privilege and disposability. The dialectic of "Global US [Israel]" and "Global Illegal Aliens [Palestine]" exemplifies this apartheid framework, with far-reaching implications for understanding modern geopolitics.

The US-Israel Geopolitical Hypostasis: Chosenness and Exclusion

At the heart of the US-Israel relationship lies a shared mythology of exceptionalism and chosenness, as Amy Kaplan has noted.[34] Both nations frame themselves as "chosen nations," divinely mandated to tame and civilize unruly frontiers. This narrative, deeply rooted in ultra-right Christian ideologies and the misappropriation of biblical texts, serves as a theological justification for policies of expansion, militarization, and exclusion. For instance, the concept of the promised land is often invoked as a divine mandate to legitimize Israel's occupation of Palestinian territories. Similarly, the doctrine of American Manifest Destiny, steeped in biblical language, was used to justify the violent displacement of Indigenous peoples in the United States, as well as the occupation of northern Mexican territories and Caribbean lands during the nineteenth and twentieth centuries.

---

33. Raheb, *Decolonizing Palestine*.
34. Kaplan, *Our American Israel*.

Raheb's work highlights how the Bible, when weaponized through ultra-right Judeo-Christian ideologies, becomes a tool to sanctify land acquisition and power consolidation. Theologies that emphasize chosenness and divine entitlement contribute to a moral framework in which the dispossession of others—whether Palestinians or Indigenous Americans—is framed not as injustice but as fulfillment of a sacred mission.[35] This ideological correspondence between "holy land" theology and state power underpins the mechanisms of global apartheid.[36]

Global US [Israel] and Global Illegal Aliens [Palestine]: A Dialectic of Apartheid

This theological and ideological framework manifests materially through the dialectic of "Global US [Israel]" and "Global Illegal Aliens [Palestine]." In this schema, "Global US [Israel]" represents the privileged axis of global power, characterized by military dominance, economic supremacy, and cultural hegemony. On the other side, "Global Illegal Aliens [Palestine]" symbolizes those relegated to disposability—stateless, marginalized, and excluded from the protections and privileges afforded to the dominant group.

In the modern state of Israel, this dialectic is evident in the systemic marginalization of Palestinians through legal discrimination, land confiscation, and the denial of basic rights. These practices have escalated to the level of state terrorism following the events of October 7, 2024, and the subsequent war in Gaza. The occupation of Palestinian territories parallels apartheid-era South Africa, where laws and policies were deliberately crafted to uphold racial and economic hierarchies. Palestinians are perpetually

---

35. Raheb, *Decolonizing Palestine*, 93–127.

36. I first encountered the concepts of "Global Israel" and "Global Palestine" during a presentation by Mitri Raheb at the American Academy of Religion in November 2024. These concepts prompted me to reflect on our contemporary world order through the framework of apartheid, viewed through the decolonial lens of colonial modernity.

rendered "illegal aliens" in their own land, denied sovereignty, and subjected to militarized control.

In the United States of America, a parallel dynamic unfolds through the treatment of racialized minorities, undocumented migrants, and Indigenous communities. Immigration policies, border militarization, and mass incarceration create a system that mirrors the exclusionary practices of Israel's occupation. The figure of the "illegal alien" in US discourse parallels the dehumanization of Palestinians, constructing an "Other" who is stripped of legitimacy and humanity. Ultra-right Judeo-Christian ideologies further reinforce this dynamic, often portraying undocumented migrants as lawbreakers who threaten the "promised land" of the United States, drawing directly on the biblical narratives that underpin these ideologies.

Land, Power, and Biblical Misuse: The Engine of Global Apartheid

Central to this global apartheid framework is the triangulation of land, power, and biblical misuse. As Mitri Raheb argues, the Bible's narratives have often been co-opted to legitimize land acquisition and the consolidation of political and military power. This misuse is evident in how Israel's settlement policies and the US's westward expansion were framed as divine mandates. These narratives not only erase the histories and rights of those dispossessed but also create a moral and theological justification for systemic exclusion.

Political ideologies rooted in religious fundamentalism—such as ultra-right evangelicalism in the US, Temple Mount activists in Israel, and Hamas in Palestine—exacerbate these dynamics. These movements reduce complex theological ideas into rigid doctrines of chosenness, entitlement, and extermination, which play a key role in sustaining systems of domination. They provide a moral veneer for displacement and militarization, aligning theological rhetoric with the material interests of power. The result is a system where the dispossession of "illegal aliens" is not only tolerated but sanctified as part of a divine plan.

A contemporary illustration of this "sanctified" plan for exclusion and domination is the so-called *Project 2025*. Crafted by US think tanks like The Heritage Foundation in anticipation of a Donald Trump victory in the 2024 election, this ultra-conservative policy agenda aims to reshape federal policies significantly. Framed as a vision to restore conservative governance, its priorities include deregulation, limited government, culturally conservative values, and centralized executive authority. Specific goals include rolling back climate policies, restricting regulatory powers, expanding Christian religious freedoms, and restructuring immigration and healthcare systems.

The potential impacts of *Project 2025* would vary widely across social and economic groups. It was poised to disproportionately harm low-income families, immigrant communities, marginalized social groups (such as LGBTQ+ individuals), and climate advocacy efforts. Conversely, it would benefit conservative Christian organizations, corporate interests, wealthy investors, and rural communities seeking energy independence. This plan epitomizes how monocultural political ideologies rooted in exclusivity consolidate power while marginalizing vulnerable groups, reinforcing the systemic separation and inequality inherent in global apartheid.

In the first 100 days of President Donald Trump's second term, his administration implemented a significant portion of the policy recommendations outlined in the Heritage Foundation's *Project 2025*. Notably, nearly 45 percent of the 126 non-tariff executive orders issued during this period closely mirrored the proposals in *Project 2025*'s "Mandate for Leadership." These actions included reinstating Schedule F to facilitate the replacement of federal employees with political appointees, dismantling diversity, equity, and inclusion (DEI) programs, initiating the dismantling of the Department of Education, and implementing policies to boost domestic energy production and strengthen immigration enforcement. Furthermore, key figures associated with *Project 2025*, such as Russ Vought and Peter Navarro, were appointed to influential positions within the administration, underscoring the alignment between the project's blueprint and the administration's early actions. This concerted effort to reshape federal governance structures and policies reflects the administration's commitment to the objectives set forth in *Project 2025*.[37]

The Fear Factor in Global Apartheid

Global apartheid operates not only through overt policies and ideologies but also through the pervasive force of fear. Fear of the "Other," fear of displacement, and fear of change are central to its social order. For privileged groups, fear dissipates as a sense of triumphalism emerges and political paralysis is reinforced—a desire to preserve the status quo amidst rapid societal shifts in politics, religion, and civic life. For marginalized communities in the Global North, when fear reaches its highest point, it often translates into civic paralysis and political conformity, born out of frustration with systemic exclusion and diminishing opportunities.

This paralyzing fear is not incidental but infused. Global apartheid thrives on a narrative of insecurity that pits communities against one another, ensuring that the social fabric remains shredded. The resulting anxiety fosters a paralyzing sense of helplessness among some and fuels social upheaval among others. Both outcomes serve to maintain the structures of global apartheid by preventing collective action and solidarity. We will explore how this dynamic transforms the oppressed into supporters of their oppressors in the next chapter.

Embracing Fear: Toward a New Framework of Christian Re-Existence

Amidst the fear perpetuated by global apartheid, there lies an opportunity to "embrace fear" as an act of faith and a catalyst for

37. Cohen, "Trump's First 100 Days;" O'Harrow Jr. et al., "Trump Reinstates Schedule F"; Heritage Foundation, *Mandate for Leadership*; Shear and Savage, "Trump Administration Pushes Education Cuts"; Korecki, "Project 2025's Architect."

transformation. Rather than allowing fear to paralyze or dominate under the monocultural logic of Babel (Gen 11), it can move us toward one another in *ekklesia*—a Spirit-empowered community of liberation based on the pluriversal logic of Pentecost (Acts 2). In this reimagining, fear (of God and injustice) becomes the starting point for fostering justice, building solidarity across divides, and transcending systems of exclusion as agents of "another world of Possible."

Communities of re-existence reject the logic of domination and separation, instead cultivating spaces of pluriversal coexistence that value diversity and mutuality. Historical and contemporary examples provide a blueprint for such transformation. The book of Acts portrays the early Christian community as one marked by radical sharing and inclusion, where differences were celebrated rather than suppressed. Similarly, the Zapatista communities and their caracoles in Chiapas, Mexico, embody a modern pluriversal experiment, embracing autonomy, collective governance, and a rejection of hierarchies imposed by global capitalism and state-centric models of power.

Reconstituting as communities of re-existence requires acknowledging the anxiety and pain that often accompany societal change. Fear, while real, need not fuel exclusion or inaction. Instead, it can empower action that dismantles global apartheid and reimagines a world order centered on equity, justice, and shared humanity. By embracing fear through the power of the Spirit, individuals and communities can transcend the paralysis of *resignation* and the destructiveness of violent unrest, by creating spaces of shared humanity that embody cognitive justice, decolonial coalitions, and missional resilience. In one sentence, the paralysis of monocultural *resignation* must be transformed into the motion of pluriversal *re-assignment!*

This chapter has sought to illuminate the mechanisms of global apartheid, deeply rooted in the enduring legacy of coloniality—against the West's own classical political wisdom—and sustained by modern theological, political, and economic systems. From the historical entanglement of land, power, and biblical misinterpretation to modern-day manifestations of systemic exclusion, the analysis reveals how structures of privilege and disposability continue to define our world order. At the core of these crises lies the normalization of monocultural ideologies operating through the Colonial Matrix of Power, privileging a narrow vision of humanity while marginalizing the majority.

To dismantle this system and heal the colonial wound, we must confront the ideological foundations that sustain global apartheid and embrace a pluriversal vision of equity, diversity, and shared humanity. This vision calls for courage, imagination, and an unwavering commitment to cognitive justice and inventive re-existence. By drawing inspiration from virtuous political wisdom, Western and Indigenous, and regenerating pluriversal experiments around the world, in the power of the Spirit, we can forge new frameworks of Christian re-existence that transverse monocultural fear to cultivate inclusive, life-giving pluriversal communities. This reimagined world is not only possible—it is under way.

Discussion Questions

For Community Organizers

- *Addressing Structural Inequality:* How does the concept of global apartheid apply to the challenges faced by marginalized communities in your context? What practical steps can be taken to challenge systems of exclusion and disposability locally and globally?
- *Mobilizing Intersectional Change:* How do race, gender, class, and other identity markers intersect to maintain systems of privilege and marginalization? How can grassroots movements effectively address these interconnections while building inclusive coalitions?
- *Fear as a Barrier and Opportunity:* Fear often manifests as either political paralysis or social unrest. How can communities

harness fear constructively to overcome divisions, resist systemic domination, and foster solidarity across boundaries?

- *Building Global Solidarity:* What specific actions can local communities take to support international movements challenging global systems of apartheid and coloniality? How can lessons from pluriversal experiments, such as the Zapatista caracoles, inform grassroots organizing?

For Faith-Based Leaders

- *Faith, Fear, and Liberation:* How can Christian leaders address the paralyzing fear that sustains global apartheid, moving instead toward a Spirit-driven community of liberation and solidarity (*ekklesia*)?

- *The Bible as a Tool for Justice:* What specific theological approaches can reinterpret the Bible to challenge systems of inequality and exclusion? How can leaders guide their congregations in this critical work?

- *Creating Inclusive Communities:* How can churches and faith-based organizations foster spaces that actively challenge systemic inequalities, promote ecological justice, and affirm human dignity across divisions?

- *Global and Local Responsibility:* What specific steps can Christian communities take to address global crises, such as the persecution of impoverished immigrants labeled "illegal aliens" in the US, Europe, and in the case of the Palestinians in the West Bank and Gaza, while staying rooted in their local contexts?

- *Missional Resilience:* In the face of political and social challenges like *Project 2025*, how can Christian communities cultivate resilience that prioritizes kingdom ethics by way of equity, inclusion, and global solidarity?

For the Classroom

- *Colonial Legacies in Modern Systems:* How has the history of coloniality shaped today's political, economic, and social hierarchies? Which historical events mentioned in the text most clearly illustrate the evolution of global apartheid?
- *Theology and Power:* Discuss the role of religious narratives in legitimizing systems of domination. How can theology be reclaimed to challenge these systems and promote justice-oriented frameworks?
- *Citizenship and Inclusion:* How do the ideas of "chosen nations" and "illegal aliens" disrupt traditional notions of citizenship and belonging? What alternative models of inclusive citizenship can be developed?
- *Reimagining Fear:* In what ways does fear reinforce or challenge systems of exclusion? How can discussions about fear be reframed to empower individuals and communities toward transformative action?
- *Pluriversal Possibilities:* How does the concept of pluriversal coexistence, as explored through the book of Acts or the Zapatista movement, provide a model for inclusive and equitable living? What barriers must be overcome to realize such frameworks in practice?

Chapter 2

Choosing the Oppressor
— Theopolitical Reflections on the Aftermath of the 2024 US Election —

FEW MOMENTS IN RECENT US history have been as perplexing as the 2024 presidential election. Large numbers of marginalized communities—Latino/a immigrants, middle-class women, African Americans, and younger millennials—rallied behind a candidate whose policies seemingly undermined their own interests. Yet, as this chapter will illustrate, this paradox is neither unprecedented nor inexplicable. Historically, we have witnessed oppressed groups form strategic alliances with dominant powers. Consider the Indian elites who supported the British Raj, or Indigenous leaders who facilitated the Spanish conquest in Abya Yala (Latin America). In each instance, the oppressed weighed their immediate survival against the long-term costs of complicity. The 2024 election, in many ways, represents a contemporary echo of these historical patterns.

To make sense of this dynamic, we begin by examining historical precedents of oppressed groups aligning with those in power—often in the hope of securing fleeting economic or social advantages. From there, we examine how *authoritarian populism* exploits unmet needs and distrust in neoliberal governance (Santos,

West). We show how weakened safety nets breed "bulldozer" leaders promising swift change, while populism can veer into totalitarianism (Arendt) and anti-establishment appeal (Chomsky). At this point, we delve into the concept of "aporophobia" to explain harsh immigration policies targeting the poor (Cortina). Many voters, abandoned by both major parties for decades, viewed Trump less as a champion of racial justice and more as a wrecking ball to the status quo—a status quo they believed had repeatedly failed them.

Strategically, we turn to Miguel De La Torre's provocative argument that "whiteness" and "Eurochristianity" are elastic constructs.[1] By adopting conservative stances—such as opposing abortion or LGBTQ+ rights—people of color and immigrants can effectively "perform whiteness," purchasing temporary proximity to power. This sociological and theological lens helps explain why certain Latino/a and Black communities rallied behind an administration widely perceived as hostile to their broader interests.

Finally, a crucial piece of this puzzle is the role of religious fundamentalism and dominion theology, particularly the rise of the New Apostolic Reformation. By casting Trump as a modern-day King Cyrus, these religious leaders nurtured a narrative of divine appointment that overshadowed concerns of racial equity or economic fairness.

Finally, this chapter concludes by asking how we might navigate fear and hope when structures of oppression appear so unyielding. Drawing on De La Torre's critiques of a naive religious "hope" that often props up empire and Santos's critique of "hope without fear and fear without hope" as a trigger to political conformity, we explore the notion of *embracing fear* on the basis of "strategic hopelessness." It is only by confronting the severity of the systemic injustice—and abandoning illusions of quick reform—that a more robust, community-centered hope might emerge as a *rumor* of re-existence. This is possible by traversing

---

1. The term "whiteness" is attributed to Franz Fanon, *Black Skin, White Masks* (1952, 1967) and *Wretched of the Earth* (1961), while George E. "Tink" Tinker is recognized for coining the term "Eurochristian." De La Torre demonstrates how Western culture, identity, and politics is pervasively embedded with these two social constructs.

fear, in the power of the Spirit, rather than yielding to fake hope in conformity to the rhetoric of imperial imagination. In short, this chapter interrogates the deeper forces at play behind marginalized support for oppressive power, revealing how history, theology, and social identity converge to produce political outcomes that, at first glance, defy conventional logic.

1. Historical Precedents of Oppressed Groups Supporting Their Oppressors: Colonial and Post-Colonial Alignments

A survey of colonial histories around the globe reveals a disconcerting pattern: communities under subjugation or threat frequently strike alliances with the very forces that subdue them. These alignments, often depicted as treachery or opportunism, are more accurately understood as pragmatic choices, forged amid crises of survival and deeply rooted local rivalries.

One emblematic example can be found in British-colonial India, where local elites—landowners, princely states, and urban aristocrats—sided with the Raj to preserve power within their regions.[2] In return, the British secured both bureaucratic efficiency and a formidable local defense system, ensuring minimal resistance from the broader populace. Historians note that these alliances were fueled by the belief that British patronage would keep communal tensions and rival potentates in check.[3] Yet this cooperation also enabled oppressive tax systems, legal double-standards, and exploitative labor arrangements that lingered long after independence, intensifying wealth disparities in rural communities.

A parallel narrative unfolded in Abya Yala (Latin America) during the Conquest, where the Tlaxcalans famously allied with Spanish conquistadors against the Aztec Empire.[4] These Indigenous groups, striving to break free from Aztec dominance, seized

---

2. Bates, *Subalterns and Raj*, 33.
3. Bates, *Subalterns and Raj*, 35.
4. Restall, *Seven Myths*, 22.

upon Spanish arrival as a strategic opportunity. Colonial records underscore how such alliances provided the Tlaxcalans with certain protections and economic privileges under the early colonial regime. However, the collaboration also facilitated European cultural suppression, missionary campaigns, and extractive labor systems that ultimately ensnared the very communities seeking liberation. As historian Matthew Restall explains, "Many Indigenous factions interpreted the arrival of the Spaniards as a chance to shift the balance of power, even if it meant trading one overlord for another."[5]

In sub-Saharan Africa, colonial administrators—especially the British—went a step further by institutionalizing "indirect rule," which deputized local chiefs to govern in the colonizers' stead.[6] Oral histories and archival documents indicate the internal tensions this arrangement created: certain chiefs, hoping to elevate their clan's standing, imposed new taxes and labor demands to please British overlords. In many cases, compliance spared their communities from heavy military reprisals—at least initially. But these newly minted "colonial chiefs" soon found themselves enmeshed in a governance structure that hollowed out traditional systems of justice and communal reciprocity, leaving a residue of hierarchical, top-down control long after independence.[7]

Taken together, these colonial and postcolonial histories serve as cautionary lessons on the intricate and often fraught pathways that oppressed groups traverse in the pursuit of stability or self-preservation. Far from simplistic betrayals, these alliances typically arose in landscapes where rebellion promised devastation, and neutrality was often impossible. They highlight how internal sociopolitical tensions—whether in the form of ethnic rivalries, inherited caste systems, or regional feuds—become fertile ground for external powers to exploit, fracturing the possibility of collective resistance.

5. Restall, *Seven Myths*, 39.
6. Mamdani, *Citizen and Subject*, 14.
7. Mamdani, *Citizen and Subject*, 17.

Choosing the Oppressor

In many ways, these colonial and postcolonial histories cast new light on the contradictions of contemporary politics. The 2024 election, in which some marginalized USAmerican voters supported policies seemingly detrimental to their long-term well-being, can be seen as the latest variation on an old theme. As with the Tlaxcalans or local Indian princes, segments of today's electorates may perceive alignment with powerful figures—despite the risks—as a strategic hedge against economic precarity, cultural marginalization, or a feared alternative.

This historical backdrop invites a more measured interpretation of why oppressed groups "choose" the oppressor: often, it is not a wholehearted endorsement of oppressive structures but a calculated gamble made in the hope of securing immediate relief or limited upward mobility. Only by reckoning with these precedents—and their enduring legacy—can we begin to understand the multilayered motives that drive modern alliances with dominant power. As with colonial intermediaries, the motivations of present-day voters—survival, aspiration, internal disunity—converge to create unexpected, seemingly paradoxical alliances that, upon closer examination, fit into a well-worn historical pattern. In the short term, faced with the void of unmet needs, opting for the oppressor is not unthinkable.

2. Authoritarian Populism, Aporophobia, and US Deportation Policies

In an era marked by stark economic inequalities and political disillusionment, *authoritarian populism* has emerged as a potent force. Social scholars of the stature of Boaventura de Sousa Santos and Cornel West both emphasize that neoliberal governance—characterized by deregulation, privatization, and the erosion of social safety nets—often fails to address the urgent material needs of marginalized communities.[8] In this void of unmet needs, charismatic strongmen can appear as "bulldozers" poised to shatter a system

---

8. Santos, *End of the Cognitive Empire*, 40–59.

widely seen as indifferent or exploitative. Disenfranchised voters, left behind by traditional political elites, thus turn to authoritarian leaders who promise swift, sweeping reforms that seem to restore moral, economic, and social order.

However, this quest for "security of progress" through strongman rule carries significant risks. Hannah Arendt warned that loneliness and social atomization create fertile ground for totalitarian ideologies, which reduce nuanced political realities to "us-versus-them" narratives and scapegoat entire groups—often immigrants or minority populations—for systemic failures.[9] In contemporary contexts, these scapegoated groups are further marginalized through the digital echo chambers where xenophobic and *aporophobic* sentiments flourish, aided by social media algorithms that amplify fearmongering rhetoric.

According to Noam Chomsky, another notable social scientist of our time, the mainstream media's narrowing of political debate can push desperate communities into the arms of authoritarian populists, whose "anti-establishment" personas resonate with those who feel betrayed by the status quo.[10] In such a milieu, figureheads like Donald Trump tap into anxieties over job insecurity, cultural change, and demographic shifts. Yet, as Cornel West cautions, the solutions offered by populist strongmen rarely address the deeper injustices of racial capitalism.[11] Instead, these leaders frequently propose draconian policies—particularly with regard to immigration—that deepen social fissures and consolidate power in ways that threaten democratic norms.

Central to understanding these draconian immigration measures is the concept of aporophobia, introduced by Spanish philosopher Adela Cortina. Aporophobia denotes an aversion or hostility toward the poor, illuminating how societal contempt for poverty can shape legislative and cultural attitudes.[12] In the United States, this is starkly visible in harsh deportation protocols. Recent US

---

9. Arendt, *Origins of Totalitarianism*, 305–24.
10. Chomsky, *Media Control*, 33–45.
11. West, *Democracy Matters*, 12–15.
12. Cortina, *Aporophobia*.

immigration enforcement actions against Haitian migrants have drawn criticism from human rights organizations, which highlight the use of Title 42 expulsions and lack of individualized asylum assessments as disproportionately affecting this group.[13] The targeting of low-income populations—whether Haitian asylum seekers, unaccompanied Central American children, Ukrainian refugees, or other impoverished migrant groups—reveals how aporophobia can operate under the auspices of "border security," perpetuating a bias against those deemed economically undesirable.[14]

Cortina's analysis sheds light on how social fear of poverty itself undergirds these measures, prioritizing immigrants who are viewed as economically beneficial while subjecting poorer applicants to heightened scrutiny.[15] In the same breath, the Dutch-American sociologist Saskia Sassen underscores that global inequalities exacerbate this bias, as nations in the Global North impose ever-tighter controls on migrants from impoverished regions in the Global South.[16] In effect, a hierarchy of desirability emerges, where those lacking financial capital or elite skill sets face systemic exclusion. In geopolitical perspective, David Harvey's work on neoliberal capitalism further contextualizes these dynamics by linking the pursuit of wealth accumulation to the marginalization of those unable to contribute profitably to the market.[17] Over time, deportation policies become a tool to expel individuals perceived as economically burdensome, illustrating the intersection of authoritarian populism's scapegoating tactics with aporophobia's stigmatization of the poor.

---

13. Human Rights Watch, "U.S. Deliberately Inflicting Harm." Also see Amnesty International, "They Did Not Treat Us Like People."

14. It is no longer just a matter of "border security"—informational surveillance is now taking place within US territory. Freedom of speech is at risk and under attack. I must note that, in preparing this work, I was forced to seek alternative sources to document data and claims after discovering that the original sources had been digitally blocked in the US by algorithmic filters.

15. Cortina, *Aporophobia*, xx.

16. Sassen, *Territory, Authority, Rights*, 277–86.

17. Harvey, *Brief History of Neoliberalism*, 67–80.

In sum, authoritarian populism flourishes in the void of unmet needs —where disillusionment with (neo)liberal governance converges with societal fears of poverty. By scapegoating economically vulnerable migrants, populist leaders offer a faux "shortcut" to security and the restoration of prosperity that often masks deeper structural inequities. Far from merely enforcing border control, these policies reveal a layered aversion to poverty that perpetuates exclusion and injustice. If the ultimate goal is a more democratic and equitable society, then addressing the aporophobic underpinnings of US deportation policies—and recognizing them as part of a broader authoritarian trend—becomes essential. To this end, elaborating on the elasticity of whiteness is key.

3. Governing the "Lesser People": The Elasticity of Whiteness

Within contemporary USAmerican politics, the seemingly contradictory alliances between people of color and overtly nationalist agendas can be partly explained by what Miguel De La Torre defines as "Eurochristianity."[18] According to De La Torre, this version of Christianity extends back to the medieval roots of European Christendom, which was shaped by crusades, colonization, and a theology of racial hierarchy. Far from being merely about religious doctrine, Eurochristianity constitutes an enduring sociopolitical structure that equates "Christian" with hegemonic power—often at odds with the liberative teachings of Jesus found in the Gospels.[19] As it developed over centuries of colonial expansion, this system normalized the idea that certain races, cultures, and nations are closer to God's favor, thereby justifying the conquest and governance of "lesser" peoples.

A key feature of Eurochristianity, De La Torre argues, is the elasticity of whiteness: a malleable social construct that can absorb new groups who adopt its fundamental premise of domination

---

18. De La Torre, *Resisting Apartheid America*, 48–49.
19. De La Torre, *Resisting Apartheid America*, 50–52.

and privileged status.[20] Over the last two centuries, various immigrant communities in the United States—Irish, Italian, Jewish—have successively gained admission into the circle of whiteness by endorsing oppressive structures, such as segregationist policies or anti-immigrant sentiment. This pattern continues today as certain segments of Black and Latino/a communities perform whiteness—embracing strict immigration enforcement, military strength, and conservative morality—to secure an elevated position within the political hierarchy.

Noel Ignatiev's historical analysis of "how the Irish became white" underscores that this assimilation into the dominant racial category frequently entails denouncing or distancing oneself from other marginalized groups, thereby solidifying a system of stratification that benefits those at the top.[21] This text provides a historical template for understanding how new immigrant groups can "move up" in a racialized system by effectively rejecting alliance with other marginalized populations. In parallel, some Latino/a groups seek acceptance through behavior or policies that mark a distance from less "assimilated" or more racialized peers. We will revisit this argument in our next chapter.

Even overtly religious dimensions of public life can reinforce this elasticity. When pastors and church leaders amplify nationalist, dominionist rhetoric—characterizing USAmerica as uniquely chosen by God—they implicitly tie the Christian faith to a framework that privileges Euroamerican norms.[22] In this schema, individuals of diverse ethnic backgrounds who buy into a Eurochristian vision of power often receive symbolic promotions in social standing. By wielding conservative theological stances (opposition to abortion, LGBTQ+ rights, or immigration leniency), they can signal conformity with a broader narrative of cultural supremacy. Such "performances of whiteness" obscure systemic injustices by suggesting that anyone, regardless of skin color, can achieve inclusion—provided they champion the status

---

20. De La Torre, *Resisting Apartheid America*, 58–60.
21. Ignatiev, *How the Irish Became White*, 81–89.
22. De La Torre, *Resisting Apartheid America*, 72–76.

quo of dominion-based Christianity. In turn, these new adherents become strong allies for political figures whose policies may, paradoxically, disadvantage the very communities to which these allies belong. Our case in point.

The Role of Religious Fundamentalism in Political Identity

Christian Nationalism as a Political Force

Christian nationalism frames Trump as a protector of USAmerica's Christian heritage, reinforcing support among white evangelicals and conservative Latino Catholics.[23] Despite Donald Trump's well-documented immoral lifestyle, multiple criminal convictions, and his frequent use of profanity and dehumanizing rhetoric, many evangelical Christians, including minorities, voted for him in 2016. They believed he would prevent the erosion of Eurochristian dominance in the United States by appointing conservative Supreme Court justices to de-legalize abortion and by building a wall to prevent illegal immigrants from bringing drugs, violence, sex trafficking, and Islamic extremist influences into the United States. In fact, a 2018 study by Paul Djupe and Ryan Burge showed that among Republicans, approval for Donald Trump directly correlated to church attendance. By 2020, a different study showed the connection between regular church attendance and Trump voters was even stronger.[24]

In a *New York Times* article titled "Why Fundamentalists Love Trump," USAmerican political commentator David French argues that Donald Trump fits in with religious fundamentalists because all forms of fundamentalism are less about what a person believes than the framework of how they believe.[25] French identifies certainty, ferocity, and solidarity as three key traits underlying

---

23. Whitehead and Perry, *Taking America Back for God*.
24. See Djupe and Burge, "Regular Churchgoing Doesn't Make Trump Voters More Moderate," and Nortey, "Most White Americans."
25. French, "Why Fundamentalists Love Trump."

fundamentalism and notes how Trumpism embodies each of them.[26] While acknowledging that not all Christians are fundamentalists, French claims that religious fundamentalists "are virtually always regular churchgoers."[27]

Embedded within religious fundamentalism is the New Apostolic Reformation (NAR), a relatively new and zealous branch of the Pentecostal-Charismatic movement that subscribes to a unique form of dominion theology popularized by NAR leaders like Bill Johnson and Lance Wallnau. Johnson is the senior leader of Bethel Church, a nondenominational megachurch in Redding, California. The congregation is internationally recognized for Bethel Music, its influential contemporary worship collective, and for operating the Bethel School of Supernatural Ministry, a certificate program that trains students in charismatic ministry such as healing and prophecy. Wallnau is the author of *God's Chaos Candidate* (2016), which predicted Donald Trump's presidency. Together, the two co-edited *Invading Babylon: The Seven Mountain Mandate* (2013). The book describes the Seven Mountain Mandate, which they present as a "revelation" from God that "helps us strategically identify different aspects of society so that cultural transformation can become a manageable task."[28] The seven mountains include religion, arts, media, business, government, family, and education.

In summary, the Seven Mountain Mandate lays out theological justification to embrace Christian nationalism, along with spiritual practices and practical strategies to advance on and dominate the seven named "mountains" of civil society. In essence, the "mandate" calls religious fundamentalists to divine active duty and emboldens them with certainty, ferocity, and solidarity to aggressively attempt to bring the nation and the world under God's reign. As in former iterations of crusade mentality, such a vision can lead power brokers to make unholy alliances.

People who embraced Wallnau's prediction of Trump's presidency appreciated the parallels he noted between Donald Trump

---

26. French, "Why Fundamentalists Love Trump."
27. French, "Why Fundamentalists Love Trump."
28. Wallnau et al., *Invading Babylon*, 12.

and King Cyrus from the Bible. King Cyrus was an ancient Persian king who conquered Babylon and thus ended Israel's Babylonian captivity by allowing the captives to return home and begin rebuilding Jerusalem, particularly the temple. When white evangelicals are confronted with Trump's moral failures, envisioning him as a modern-day Cyrus gives some of them biblical justification to offer him their unwavering support. They may not believe Trump is one of them. Instead, they view him as a secular king who is sympathetic to their cause. They give him their loyalty because they expect, in turn, to have his ear and support to impose (or re-impose) Eurochristian norms on USAmerican society.

The NAR intensified the widespread acceptance of Christian nationalist thinking among white evangelicals by fusing the Seven Mountain Mandate's dominionist eschatology with fearful rhetoric about an alleged attack on religious freedom, the potential moral ramifications of abortion, the LGBTQ+ "agenda," and threats posed by illegal immigration, such as drug trafficking, human trafficking, and violent crime. The Trump campaign amplified the fear rhetoric as the NAR's influence continued to grow, crossing racial demographics and denominations, including Catholicism, while continuing to be most prominently represented among the Pentecostal-Charismatic Movement, which is often cited as the fastest-growing form of Christianity in the world.

Although the NAR variant of Christian nationalism is directly related to the Seven Mountain Mandate, its modern origins might be traced to the intersection of the Charismatic, Latter Rain, and Moral Majority movements alongside the National Day of Prayer in the United States. By participating in "Jericho Marches," inspirational religious conferences, and worship protests endorsed by Neo-Charismatic figures who endorsed Trump, some people believed they were engaging in spiritual warfare against a satanic takeover of a nation they believed God had established and ordained to Christianize the world. In *The Violent Take It By Force* (2024), Matthew Taylor outlines how key NAR leaders influenced significant government officials and their constituents in the months leading up to the January 6, 2021 attack on the United

States Capitol. He profiles Paula White, C. Peter Wagner, Cindy Jacobs, Che Ahn, Lance Wallnau, Sean Feucht, and Dutch Sheets as key figures who fostered Trumpian Christian fundamentalism. With the exception of Che Ahn (a Korean USAmerican megachurch pastor and protégé of Peter Wagner, the former Fuller Theological Seminary professor who named and helped mastermind the New Apostolic Reformation), Taylor's groundbreaking book highlights important white political influencers within the NAR, but overlooks significant minority group leaders, especially first-generation immigrants, dual citizens, and Native USAmericans. The most influential leader of a minority group associated with the NAR may be Rev. Samuel Rodriguez, who has served in advisory roles for multiple United States presidents and leads the National Hispanic Christian Leadership Conference (NHCLC), one of the largest Latino Christian organizations in the United States. In December 2024, Rodriguez, a Pentecostal pastor of Puerto Rican descent, celebrated the record-breaking number of Hispanic USAmericans who voted for Trump and was looking forward to the president-elect deporting illegal immigrants and closing the southern borders.[29]

Miguel De La Torre and Resisting Apartheid America

It may seem counterintuitive for evangelical minorities like Rodriguez to politically align with an opportunist authoritarian populist leader known to perpetuate racist and sexist tropes, especially when Rodriguez regularly claims to be a justice activist following the example of Martin Luther King Jr. However, Miguel De La Torre critiques religious fundamentalism as an ideological tool that justifies oppression, arguing that it conditions believers to accept systemic injustice under the guise of divine will.[30] According to De La Torre, in the 2024 election, this framework was instrumental in mobilizing Latino evangelicals toward conservative nationalism.

---

29. Rodriguez, "Hispanic Voters."
30. De La Torre, *Resisting Apartheid America*, 50–73.

However, when asked about the political shift among Hispanic voters in 2024, Rev. Rodriguez named inflation, the continuum of lawlessness (including open borders), and parental rights as the "trifecta" of concerns driving Latino/a voters.[31] In an interview with Mike Huckabee, Rodriguez elaborated.

> Why did Latinos shift so hard to the right? Well, because we . . . it's part of who we are. We are faith, family, and freedom. The Latino community basically said the following to the Democratic establishment. "Get your hands off our children. Stop attempting to indoctrinate them."[32]

In addition to addressing parental rights, Rodriguez said Latinos voted against violence, drug addiction, and human trafficking tied to Mexican drug cartels. Then, he pointed out the disproportionate number of Hispanic/Latino USAmericans who serve or have served in the US military versus other racial demographics, claiming that Latino USAmericans are exceptionally patriotic citizens. He ended his remarks by implying that it was ridiculous and offensive for an MSNBC host to suggest racism was a contributing factor behind 56 percent of Hispanic males voting for Donald Trump in 2024.

De La Torre's theories about the elasticity of whiteness and Eurochristianity push back on Rodriguez's claim that Latino males who voted for Trump weren't being racist. When "whiteness" is conceived not as a skin complexion but a social construct that can subsume people of all ethnicities, and Eurochristianity is seen more as an on-ramp to sociopolitical power rather than a commitment to the teachings of Jesus, it is possible for Hispanic males or any other minorities to be racist and to use Eurochristian logic to justify their racism.[33] As Hispanic/Latino men attempt to gain social clout by aligning with white Eurochristian oppressors rather than the oppressed, to De La Torre's thinking, they help perpetuate

---

31. Rodriguez, "Hispanic Voters"; Martin, "Hispanic Evangelical Leader."
32. Rodriguez, "Hispanic Voters."
33. De La Torre, *Resisting Apartheid America*, 58.

"white" Eurochristian nationalism. Rodriguez, for example, illustrates De La Torre's theories in his response to the Trump administration's ICE raids on Latino churches and communities.

By presenting Latino USAmericans as exceptional patriots and claiming that the Trump administration will not target those "who are God-fearing, hard-working, not living off government subsidies, whose kids were born here,"[34] Rodriguez discourages resistance by calming the community and encouraging conformity to neoliberal, Eurochristian nationalist logic. Likewise, when Rodriguez mentions disagreement with the president's tactics alongside his intention to remind Trump's administration that evangelical Latino's helped secure Trump's presidency, he signals an expectation for reciprocity and complicity in political power broking.

Within a Christian nationalist framework, the term *Christian* can be applied to atheists, Muslims, Buddhists, Jews, and any other belief system that attaches to an iteration of Christianity that only seeks to dominate rather than align with the teachings of Jesus regarding the treatment of the poor, the sick, outcasts, strangers, enemies, the vulnerable, and others. That's why De La Torre uses the term "Eurochristian" to describe a social system that was built on racial hierarchy theories rooted in Medieval European thought and perpetuated by a callous and colonizing governing system that subjugated, enslaved, murdered, and abused people under the guise of Christian evangelism and forced adherence to Eurochristian morals and norms. This white Eurochristian paradigm, which Walter Mignolo would call the Colonial Matrix of Power, provides minority populations with opportunities to become complicit in social systems that perpetuate "white" supremacy/dominance despite knowing the potential ramifications for people on the underside of this Eurochristian agenda.

Racial (neoliberal) capitalism has been a remarkably effective tool for advancing the global reach and political power of white Eurochristian nationalism, and Donald Trump may be its most emblematic representation. Interestingly, his rise to political

---

34. Rodriguez, "Trump's Mass Deportation Plan?"

power has paralleled the rise of the New Apostolic Reformation and the dawn of a new neoliberal reformation that is bending toward authoritarian populism. Economist Joseph Stiglitz explains that neoliberal capitalism is failing because it began with the faulty premise that no one has power. Of course, within the Colonial Matrix of Power, propped up by Eurochristian whiteness, the free market may seem to offer equal opportunity for anyone willing to put in the work, but some people always begin with more power than others and quickly generate more social and political influence by exploiting the needy to increase their economic capital. As Isaiah Berlin puts it, when faced with such a scenario, "Freedom for the wolves has often meant death for the sheep."[35]

Yet, the idea of starting with nothing and working toward success is embedded in the fabric of USAmerican sensibilities. It is the essence of the USAmerican dream and continues to resonate within scrappy populist frameworks. Vijay Prashad describes Trump as "a product of the neoliberal compact. He is Frankenstein's monster."[36] Trump presents himself as a self-made billionaire living the ultimate USAmerican dream built on his capacity to work the neoliberal capitalist system to enrich himself. Yet, Prashad notes, "His claim of being a self-made billionaire is as realistic as his claim of being a self-made politician; in both arenas, he was propelled by forces far bigger than him."[37] Simultaneously, Trump plays the role of Cyrus, the charismatic king, ally, and defender of Eurochristian whiteness who matches the certainty, ferocity, and solidarity of religious fundamentalism espoused by groups like the NAR. Perhaps they are attracted to each other because each sees a refraction of self in the other.

On such an unlevel playing field, outsiders can rarely rely on talent alone and may have to hustle, strategize, and scheme their way to the top. De La Torre notes the prominence of a trickster character among stories passed down in Indigenous cultures, including Judaism. For example, consider the stories of Jacob and

---

35. Berlin, *Four Essays on Liberty*, 50.
36. Prashad, "Dr. Victor Frankenstein."
37. Prashad, "Dr. Victor Frankenstein."

Jael in the Scriptures. The trickster finds a way to outsmart the power dynamics that are designed to keep him or her subjugated. In the past, marginalized people have successfully employed trickster strategies to get ahead, but like Jacob encountering Laban as an ultimate trickster, Donald Trump may play the ultimate trickster to his base. Though some have hoped to gain respectability, social influence, or even spiritual dominion by hitching their aspirations on Donald Trump's relentless pursuit of power, they may, instead, find themselves hustled, hopeless, and hollowed out.

Or perhaps the master trickster of our time ends up being tricked by an unexpected intervention, just as it happens in the narrative of Genesis 11 (the Tower of Babel). This means that the story of triumphant hope of the moment may turn out to be also the story of strategic hopelessness performed by those embracing fear and making the fear of the Lord and fear of social injustice the most unexpected weapon of action and disruption.

Whose Hope[lessness]: Friday, Saturday, or Sunday Workers?

In a time when "fascism 2.0" is triggering "democratic involution" in forward democratic contexts like the United States,[38] Miguel A. De La Torre, in *Embracing Hopelessness*, presents a theology that challenges the common discourse on hope as a virtue, particularly as it is framed within Christian eschatology. By positioning the disenfranchised within the liminal space of Holy Saturday, De La Torre deconstructs the dominant narrative of redemptive suffering and instead calls for an ethical praxis rooted in the reality of hopelessness. This chapter ends by exploring the metaphorical categorization of justice workers—Friday workers, Saturday workers, and Sunday workers. We will proceed by critically examining the implications of De La Torres's theology of hopelessness, both

38. Santos, "Fascism 2.0."

as a critique of oppressive structures and as a potential avenue for constructing an ethical response of resiliency to injustice.[39]

Friday Workers: Crucified by the Empire

Friday workers represent those who are victims of systemic oppression, bearing the brunt of violence, economic disenfranchisement, and social marginalization. In De La Torre's theology, these workers experience the brutality of Good Friday—where the forces of empire execute dissenters and the dispossessed are left abandoned.[40] He argues that Friday workers are not simply passive sufferers but rather individuals whose existence is continually crucified by an unjust system that requires their subjugation for the preservation of privilege.[41]

De La Torre critiques the notion that Friday workers should hope for a better future, as this hope, he contends, is a luxury afforded only to those not trapped in cycles of suffering. Instead of clinging to a false optimism that often serves to maintain the status quo, Friday workers must confront their reality with an awareness that their suffering will not necessarily lead to redemption or justice.[42] This position is particularly challenging to traditional Christian theology, which frequently frames suffering as meaningful within a divine plan. De La Torre disrupts this assumption, forcing a confrontation with the stark reality that, for many, Good Friday never ends.[43]

Saturday Workers: The Space of Hopelessness

The disenfranchised exist not in the promised victory of Sunday but in the inescapable despair of Saturday. De La Torre describes

39. De La Torre, *Embracing Hopelessness*, xiii–xv.
40. De La Torre, *Embracing Hopelessness*, 4–5.
41. De La Torre, *Embracing Hopelessness*, 5–6.
42. De La Torre, *Embracing Hopelessness*, 65.
43. De La Torre, *Embracing Hopelessness*, 61–65.

Holy Saturday as the day after the crucifixion, where hope for resurrection remains uncertain, if not completely lost.[44] Saturday workers exist in this liminal space, neither fully dead nor fully alive, trapped within an economic, political, and social stasis that renders forward movement impossible.

For De La Torre, Saturday workers embody the rejection of false hope. They are those who recognize that traditional avenues for justice—electoral politics, institutional reform, or appeals to morality—have largely failed. Instead of pacifying themselves with the hope of an eventual breakthrough, Saturday workers embrace hopelessness as a radical stance.[45] Rather than seeing hopelessness as despair, De La Torre reframes it as an act of defiance. It is through this embrace of hopelessness that Saturday workers reject the illusions imposed by those who benefit from their suffering.[46]

However, the challenge inherent in De La Torre's position is how one moves beyond Saturday without falling into paralysis. If hope is dismissed entirely, does that not lead to nihilism? Here, De La Torre's constructive contribution becomes evident: hopelessness is not the end, but the means by which a new form of ethical resistance emerges.[47] By refusing to be sedated by empty promises, Saturday workers can engage in acts of defiance that expose and disrupt structures of oppression.[48]

Sunday Workers: The Privilege of Resurrection

Sunday workers, in contrast, are those who benefit from the illusion of progress. They are often those in positions of privilege who preach patience, urging the oppressed to wait for justice in an eschatological future.[49] For De La Torre, the very idea of a promised Sunday—a day of resurrection and renewal—can become a

---

44. De La Torre, *Embracing Hopelessness*, 4–5.
45. De La Torre, *Embracing Hopelessness*, 49–50.
46. De La Torre, *Embracing Hopelessness*, 49.
47. De La Torre, *Embracing Hopelessness*, 64–65.
48. De La Torre, *Embracing Hopelessness*, 52.
49. De La Torre, *Embracing Hopelessness*, 48–49.

tool of oppression when wielded as a means to pacify resistance. The dominant Christian narrative suggests that suffering will be redeemed, that justice will be realized in the fullness of time, and that the crucifixion will always be followed by resurrection. However, De La Torre argues that for the vast majority of the world's poor and disenfranchised, Sunday never comes.[50]

The critique of Sunday workers extends beyond religious discourse into the realm of social and political activism. Many well-intentioned reformers advocate for gradual progress, but such incrementalism often serves to maintain oppressive systems rather than dismantle them.[51] De La Torre's theology of hopelessness calls out this complicity, arguing that the illusion of hope can be more dangerous than despair itself. It is those who are convinced that justice will *eventually* arrive who are least likely to take radical action to make it happen.[52]

Epilogue: Daybreak Workers and the Ministry of Re-Existence

I belong to an immigrant community—and a church—that typically goes to bed late and wakes up early, at daybreak, to earn a living and keep the wheels of the US economy turning day by day. This labor allows the most privileged (the 1 percent) to live comfortably and to wake up ready for the Sunday morning sermon on hope. Interestingly, in the same facility where my congregation (and many others) worships and preaches, we encounter two diametrically different sermons. One is the "Sunday workers'" sermon on hope, offered upstairs in the "main" sanctuary for the "main" people; the other is the "Daybreak workers'" sermon in the underground basement, standing in solidarity with crucified communities—those persecuted, displaced, and vilified by imperial rhetorics of different political administrations, as well as those trapped in impotence and depression (of the Saturday) while their

---

50. De La Torre, *Embracing Hopelessness*, 61–65.
51. De La Torre, *Embracing Hopelessness*, 47, 60.
52. De La Torre, *Embracing Hopelessness*, 51–52.

loved ones are tormented by racism, sexism, aporophobia, xenophobia, and white supremacy.

The basement sermons in my church—both collective and individual—tend to combine lament, prophetic denunciation, pastoral accompaniment, and a biblical anticipation that another church and another world are possible here, now, among those who struggle, in the power of the Spirit. We do not emphasize "Sunday-hoping resurrection" themes that act as tranquilizers of the conscience—an idea De La Torre critiques. Instead, we are learning to resist in Christ, within the horizon of re-existence in the Spirit. This is a liminal space where we cultivate resilience at the borders of imperial rhetoric—somewhere between progress and triumphalism on the one hand, and defeat, pessimism, and conformity on the other. It is inevitably a border Christian life, preached with a border Christian sermon, embodying a praxis of resisting and re-existing at daybreak—on the underside and underground of history and territory.

De La Torre's perspective on hopelessness is not intimidating to us *because we do not live solely within the fragmented timeline of Friday, Saturday, and Sunday; we inhabit the in-between times, spaces, and kingdom possibilities in the power of the Spirit.* We are believers *where* we live, think, sense, act, imagine. It is not a linear timeline (of Christendom) that guides us, but rather a communal kingdom energy whose ecology subverts imperial social orders. Children, women, and people with (dis)abilities lead the way. Our identity embraces a multilingual, intercultural, intergenerational, and interpolitical posture, with shared, dialogical, and plural leadership. Clearly, we are far from "exemplary," but we remain committed to anti-racist, anti-classist, anti-sexist, and countercolonial ideologies, structures, and principles.

When it comes to the Easter story, we are like the women on the margins of the story. We stay by the cross on Friday. On Saturday, we do not let despair overtake us. Despite our grief, we continue to work through the night because we must. There is work to do, even if serving only means standing in the dark and waiting for daybreak so we can go to the tomb to care for the dead.

We do not go expecting a miracle. We go to offer tender love and respect, but if, like Mary, we find Jesus there, in the presence of a stranger, we rejoice and spread rumors of resurrection.

For churches like ours, De La Torre's rejection of hope is not a call to despair but an invitation to radical praxis. Embracing hopelessness allows the disenfranchised to break free from illusions that stifle meaningful resistance.[53] This does not entail abandoning ethical action but rather reframing its foundation. Instead of acting out of hope for a favorable outcome, De La Torre calls us to act out of necessity—to fight for justice not because we expect victory, but because it is the "only" ethical choice.[54]

This perspective challenges the reader to reconsider faith and activism. If change does not come from awaiting the proverbial Sunday, it must emerge from an uncompromising engagement with the present. Such engagement does not demand optimism; it demands steadfast commitment to struggle regardless of success's likelihood. In this respect, De La Torre's theology resonates with other radical movements that champion action without the assurance of triumph, akin to existentialist ethics or liberation theology's preferential option for the poor.[55]

In conclusion, the metaphors of Friday, Saturday, and Sunday workers serve as a potent lens for understanding De La Torre's theology of hopelessness. In the context of Western dominant views of Christian churches, *Friday workers* shoulder the burden of oppression, *Saturday workers* occupy the liminal space of despair, and *Sunday workers* benefit from the illusion of progress. But this social imaginary, although widespread, is not the only one. There are alternative ecclesial imaginations that interact with the biblical text in pertinent ethical ways, the Daybreak workers, which do not live solely within the fragmented timeline of Friday, Saturday, and Sunday. They inhabit the in-between times, spaces, and kingdom possibilities as counter–colonial-imperial spaces of re-existence, by the power of the Spirit.

---

53. De La Torre, *Embracing Hopelessness*, 60–63.
54. De La Torre, *Embracing Hopelessness*, 65–67.
55. De La Torre, *Embracing Hopelessness*, 74–75.

Discussion Questions

For Community Organizers

- *Historical Alliances and Strategic Survival:* How can the chapter's discussion of oppressed groups aligning with their oppressors—as a strategy for immediate survival—inform our work in building alliances that truly empower communities today?

- *Identifying and Countering Authoritarian Populism:* In what ways do local policies and rhetoric reflect the dynamics of authoritarian populism and aporophobia discussed in the chapter, and how can community organizers work to address and dismantle these forces?

- *Internalized Oppression and the Elasticity of Whiteness:* How does the concept of "elasticity of whiteness" help us understand divisions within marginalized communities, and what strategies might be effective in fostering genuine solidarity against systemic injustice?

- *Embracing Strategic Hopelessness:* The chapter contrasts "false hope" with radical praxis. How can the idea of "strategic hopelessness" inspire community organizing efforts that prioritize immediate, transformative action over waiting for gradual change?

For Faith-Based Leaders

- *Rethinking Hope in Ministry:* How can faith-based leaders reconcile traditional religious teachings on hope with García-Johnson and De La Torre's call for "strategic hopelessness" as a form of resistance against systemic injustice, and what implications does this have for spiritual care?

- *Challenging Internal Narratives of Identity:* In light of the chapter's discussion on the "elasticity of whiteness," how should church leaders address the ways in which certain groups may adopt oppressive norms to gain social acceptance within religious communities?

- *Faith, Politics, and the Danger of False Certainty:* How can faith-based leaders help congregants critically examine the use of religious narratives—such as portraying political figures as divinely appointed—to justify policies that may harm marginalized communities?

- *Ministry in the Margins:* Reflecting on the metaphors of Friday, Saturday, and Sunday workers, what practical steps can churches take to minister to those who feel abandoned by conventional promises of redemption, and how can they cultivate a community of resistance and re-existence in the Spirit?

For the Classroom

- *Historical Parallels in Political Alliances:* How does comparing historical alliances (like those in colonial India or Abya Yala) with modern political behavior deepen our understanding of why marginalized groups might support policies that seem counter to their long-term interests?

- *Populism and the Politics of Fear:* What role do unmet needs and societal fears play in the rise of authoritarian populism, and how can we critically analyze the impact of aporophobia on both immigration policies and political choices?

- *The Social Construction of Racial Identity:* How does the idea of "elasticity of whiteness" challenge conventional narratives about race and identity, and what implications does this have for our understanding of political behavior among diverse communities?

- *Reconceptualizing Hope in Political Theology:* In what ways does De La Torre's theology of hopelessness—and the metaphors of Friday, Saturday, and Sunday workers—challenge traditional Christian notions of hope, and how can this perspective be critically engaged within academic discussions on social justice?

Chapter 3

Political Conformity and the Crisis of Democracy
—Authoritarian Populism as the Political and Theological Challenge of Our Time—

"Case by case, we find that conformity is the easy way, and the path to privilege and prestige; dissidence carries personal costs that may be severe, even in a society that lacks such means of control as death squads, psychiatric prisons, or extermination camps.
The very structure of the media is designed to induce conformity to established doctrine."—*Noam Chomsky*[1]

The New Authoritarianism — Faith, Freedom, and the Future of Democracy

IN RECENT YEARS, SEVERAL democracies have experienced a shift toward authoritarian populism, where elected leaders exploit democratic institutions to concentrate power, weaken opposition, and restrict civil liberties while maintaining the façade of electoral competition. This phenomenon aligns with what Steven Levitsky

---

1. Chomsky, *Necessary Illusions*, 10.

and Lucan Way define as competitive authoritarianism—a regime type that retains democratic institutions but systematically undermines fair competition.[2]

Although some scholars draw parallels between contemporary authoritarian populism and historical fascism, others caution against oversimplified comparisons. For instance, David Art argues that nativism and competitive authoritarianism, rather than classical fascism, better describe the political transformations in countries like Hungary and the United States.[3] However, Gábor Halmai warns that populist leaders use constitutional manipulation—particularly in Hungary and Poland—to erode democracy from within, an approach distinct from but functionally similar to historical fascist tactics.[4] Most recently, it is not an Eastern European nation or a "third world" country that is exhibiting this antisocial democratic approach, but the United States of America under the authoritarian leadership of Donald Trump.

For some time, scholars in the field of political theory have asserted that "Latin America is the land of populism."[5] It has been observed that since the 1930s and 1940s, various forms of populism—classical, neoliberal, and radical—have emerged across the region. Additionally, the "linkage" between strong populist leaders and their followers has been attributed to four key modes of interaction: populist organizations, clientelism, mass media, and populist discourse.[6]

While this framework may accurately describe certain periods and regions in Latin America's political history, it can no longer be regarded as exclusive to the region. The characteristics and mechanisms of populism have increasingly manifested in other global contexts, challenging the notion of Latin American exceptionalism in this regard. This trend is now particularly evident in Hungary, Poland, Turkey, Brazil, El Salvador, Argentina, India,

2. Levitsky and Way, "New Competitive Authoritarianism."
3. Art, "Myth of Global Populism."
4. Halmai, "Populism, Authoritarianism, and Constitutionalism."
5. De La Torre, "Populism in Latin America," 195.
6. De La Torre, "Populism in Latin America," 203.

Israel, and the United States, where leaders have weaponized electoral victories to justify democratic backsliding.

In Turkey, for instance, Recep Tayyip Erdoğan's Justice and Development Party (AKP) has weakened judicial independence, repressed opposition, and consolidated executive power, fitting the model of competitive authoritarianism.[7] Similarly, Narendra Modi's administration in India has used majoritarian populism and religious nationalism to curtail dissent and reshape democratic norms.[8] In El Salvador, Nayib Bukele's government has actively dismantled judicial checks on executive power, signaling a rapid democratic decline.[9] In the modern state of Israel, Benjamin Netanyahu employs ethno-nationalist populism, positioning himself as the protector of Jewish identity and Western civilization while portraying Palestinians and political opponents as existential threats. His rhetoric aligns with the global populist right, including leaders like Trump, Modi, and Bolsonaro.[10]

At the present, the US administration of Donald Trump vividly exemplifies authoritarian populism, particularly through his aggressive international trade policies, including widespread tariffs imposed on key economic allies and competitors. Trump's tariff policies have been justified with nationalist rhetoric, presenting global trade as a zero-sum game that positions the US against purportedly exploitative international partners. Such measures not only appeal directly to populist sentiments by promising economic protectionism and reviving domestic industries, but also strengthen executive authority by bypassing traditional institutional checks, such as legislative oversight or international trade bodies. It is not an overstatement to say that Trump's unilateral use of tariffs exemplifies a populist strategy of mobilizing public support through nationalistic economic measures while simultaneously undermining multilateral cooperation and institutional

7. Castaldo, "Populism and Competitive Authoritarianism in Turkey."
8. Das and Mathew, "India after Modi."
9. Corrales, "Why Populism is the Sugar, Salt."
10. Gal, "Challenges of an Ethnic-Democracy."

stability, both characteristic moves within authoritarian populist governance. While some scholars argue that competitive authoritarian regimes remain unstable and prone to either democratic restoration or full autocratization,[11] others contend that authoritarian populists deliberately blur the line between democracy and autocracy to maintain legitimacy while consolidating control.[12] As democratic backsliding continues, scholars increasingly warn that authoritarian populism is not merely a deviation from democracy but a distinct political strategy capable of reshaping governance in lasting ways.[13]

How to Understand Populist Fascism and the Siege of Democracy

The renown epistemologist and social theorist from the University of Coimbra and University of Wisconsin, Boaventura de Sousa Santos, refers to this re-emergence of global populism as "populist fascism" or "social fascism" and cites as evidence the surprising election and authoritarian leadership of world figures such as Donald Trump in the United States, Jair Messias Bolsonaro in Brazil, the Brexit incident in the United Kingdom. A framing question is *in what manner is this democratic regression manifesting in the American continent and other global settings*? According to Santos, it occurs through three negations.

These negations are blurring the formal democracy that has been built since the post-independence era and are manifesting in despotisms and fascisms even in the so-called developed countries, Santos asserts. Added to this is the predominance of the state of exception or emergency—which possesses the power to suspend the constitutional rights of citizens for reasons of surveillance and national security—except that the state of exception has

---

11. Carothers, "Surprising Instability of Competitive Authoritarianism."
12. Levitsky and Way, "New Competitive Authoritarianism," 55.
13. Halmai, "Populism, Authoritarianism, and Constitutionalism," 310–11.

exceptionally become a permanent condition, in which citizens' rights remain in force but may be suspended by the state at any time. According to Santos, the following three negations manifesting democratic erosion or involution are as follows:

1. The negation of democracy through a social state occupied by antisocial capitalism.

The "liberal" democracy being proposed by *populist fascist political leaders* facilitates the granting of citizen rights vis-à-vis the private capitalist sector now falls into the hands of neoliberalism, whose economic vision determines and subjugates the social function. This is best exemplified by the administration and democratic elections of November 2020 (and 2024) in the United States of America. In an anti-Trump struggle, the majority of USAmerican citizens decided to remove Donald Trump from the presidency, thereby ending his first term, his four years of autocratic leadership (2017–2020). Yet, in an unprecedented act that astonished the nation and the world, Trump refused to accept the national vote and vetoed the democratic process—the will of the USAmerican majority—and attempted in various ways to litigate his loss in state and higher courts, alleging fraud.

The populist-fascist power of Trumpism was clearly manifested once again in its efforts to invalidate the popular vote, calling on its base to engage in civil disobedience when his attempt to contest his re-election in the state and higher courts failed. For a little while, the vast majority of the nation conformed to a political vision that portrayed Donald Trump not as a president working for the nation, but rather that the USAmerican nation was working for him.

During those days, Santos wrote an article titled "Fascism 2.0: An Intensive Course," in which he claimed that we were witnessing a unique moment in the case of the president of the world's most powerful country.[14] He identified eight symptoms in the pathology of Trump-type Fascism 2.0 in the world:

1. Do not recognize unfavorable election results,
2. Turn majorities into minorities,
3. Double standards,
4. Never speak or rule with country in mind, but always and only with your social base in mind,
5. Reality does not exist (i.e., constructing "fake news"),
6. Resentment is your most precious political resource,
7. Traditional politics is your best unknowing ally,
8. And always, always polarize.

For many US voters at that time, retiring Donald Trump from the presidency seemed the right course to uphold the nation's democratic values. Yet, Santos's notion of Trump-type fascism never truly vanished from the public imagination—it only grew stronger.

2. The negation of democracy as the denial of the citizen

The negation of democracy is manifesting through the abandonment of conditions where citizens are safe and free, in favor of regimes of surveillance imposed under the guise of national security. In this context, citizens are cast as subjects under constant suspicion by the state, which vigilantly monitors them. Today, in many parts of the world, citizens no longer trust governmental, judicial, and executive structures. Nor do these structures uphold citizens' rights.

Instead, they are perceived not as sociopolitical or civic instruments serving the populace but as mechanisms to regulate and subject them to the processes of capitalization by public and private sectors. This situation is further complicated by political

14. Santos, "Fascism 2.0."

ideologies, such as Christian nationalism and white supremacy, permeating authoritarian political administrations, policymaking, and power structures. These ideologies often intertwine, promoting exclusionary practices and undermining democratic principles.

3. The negation of democracy through governments that embrace social fascism and make democracy unnecessary

Embracing social fascism, from Santos's perspective, is transforming the state into a regime defined by profoundly unequal power dynamics and relations, which result in especially severe and potentially irreversible forms of exclusion. In this manner, a new hegemonic space-time emerges, permeating all social, economic, political, and cultural relations, thus becoming common to both state and non-state actions. As Santos poignantly expresses, "It is a time of fear . . . of the voiding of democracy . . . of social fascism in the guise of racism and violence against women, of the mercantilization of knowledge and religion."[15]

After this analysis, we arrive at two conclusions. First, the analysis reveals a trending regression of Western democracy across the American continent and others. The subversion of democratic institutions by antisocial capitalism has transformed state structures into mechanisms that prioritize neoliberal interests over the public good. Concurrently, the abandonment of a condition in which citizens are safe and free has given way to pervasive surveillance regimes that cast individuals as perpetual subjects of state suspicion, eroding trust in governmental, judicial, and executive bodies. Moreover, the embrace of social fascism—characterized by starkly unequal power dynamics and irreversible forms of exclusion—has generated a new hegemonic space-time that permeates all realms of society.

Second, the emergence of Trumpism in the US is a remarkable illustration of liberal democracy regressing by embracing

---

15. Santos, *End of the Cognitive Empire*, 266.

social fascism. For many US voters, removing Donald Trump from the presidency after his first term seemed the right course of action to uphold the nation's democratic values. Like a scene from a biblical fiction novel echoing Revelation 13:3—"One of the heads of the beast seemed to have had a fatal wound, but the fatal wound had been healed. The whole world was filled with wonder and followed the beast"—Trumpism made a dramatic return in the 2024 US elections, proving both effective and dominant against all odds. If we take Santos's analysis seriously, we must acknowledge that we are currently living under the pathology of Trump-type fascism 2.0—a phenomenon that will hurt us regardless of our political preferences, break us, and remake our society.[16]

How and Why Do We Conform to Authoritarian Populism (Fascism 2.0)?

So far, we have demonstrated that populist authoritarian leadership (Fascism 2.0) is neither monolithic nor confined to a single region or historical moment. Rather, it is a globally ascendant phenomenon that reemerges more forcefully each time in various forms—classical, neoliberal, radical, and ethno-national—across the political spectrum (left, center, right) while using evolving tactics of mass communication and control (populist organizations, clientelism, mass media, and populist discourse). In order to thrive, such leadership must reshape traditional democratic channels and bend the juridical texture of the nation-state.

Yet the public imagination of those who opt—politically and religiously—for this kind of leadership is also pivotal. In many contexts, authoritarian populism appears as the most viable alternative amid perceived moral chaos, economic turmoil, and

16. Big surprise! Too many supporters of authoritarian populist leaders, like in the case of the 2024 US elections, get surprised by unintended consequences. For instance, several segments who supported Donald Trump during the 2024 US elections were pragmatic and thought they could use Trump to hurt their opponents. They never thought Trump's policies could turn against themselves. See Graham, "Trump Supporters Who Didn't Take Him at His Word."

political instability. It thus becomes crucial to explore how and why political conformity occurs, and even more intriguing, why the very groups most vulnerable to authoritarian populism might deliberately choose such a path.

Sociocultural Frameworks for Understanding Political Conformity

In a growing global context of authoritarian populism, it becomes vital to understand how political conformity occurs—particularly how and why marginalized populations embrace seemingly detrimental political agendas. Scholars have developed multiple models to explain why individuals and groups conform politically. None of the frameworks we will present explain the full complexity of political conformity, and each of them is biased geopolitically and cognitively. Nonetheless, each framework illuminates different mechanisms and outcomes, especially among minority populations under authoritarian leadership. As we have anticipated already, political conformity—the process by which individuals or groups align their beliefs, behaviors, or attitudes with dominant political norms—remains central to the study of power and authoritarian leadership.

In seemingly democratic-forward societies experiencing neo-authoritarian political and religious leadership, minoritized populations often navigate a complex interplay between self-preservation and identity assertion. Increasingly, this dynamic is also mediated by religious ideologies. In the United States, for example, the rise of Christian nationalism and the influence of Christian Zionism encoded by white normativity have become significant factors that shape political behavior and foster conformity, sometimes at the expense of dissenting voices.

Normative and Informational Social Influence

Normative social influence posits that individuals conform to secure social acceptance or avoid sanctions. In politically charged environments, members from minority groups may adopt dominant political behaviors or narratives to avoid marginalization.[17] In contrast, informational social influence suggests that when individuals are uncertain, they look to others for guidance; in authoritarian settings, members of minorities may defer to majority behaviors perceived as more knowledgeable or legitimate.[18]

Social Identity Theory

Social identity theory, as developed by Henri Tajfel and John Turner, argues that an individual's self-concept derives in part from membership in social groups.[19] In political contexts, members from minority groups might align with dominant parties or ideologies to reinforce group identity—even when such parties have not historically championed their specific interests. This dynamic is complicated when religious identity enters the equation, as shared religious narratives can both include and exclude certain groups.

Rational Choice Theory

According to rational choice theory, political behavior results from individuals weighing costs and benefits.[20] Members from minority groups may align with dominant political structures when the expected benefits—such as economic incentives or protection from discrimination—outweigh the ideological costs.

---

17. Asch, "Opinions and Social Pressure."
18. Asch, "Opinions and Social Pressure."
19. Tajfel and Turner, "An Integrative Theory."
20. Downs, *An Economic Theory*, 6–11.

This approach, however, may oversimplify decisions that are also informed by cultural and emotional factors.

Cognitive Dissonance Theory

Leon Festinger's cognitive dissonance theory explains that individuals experience discomfort when their beliefs and behaviors are inconsistent.[21] Faced with a dominant political ideology that conflicts with their own views, minority members may gradually adjust their attitudes to reduce internal tension, sometimes internalizing repressive norms as a coping mechanism.

Structural Functionalism

From the perspective of structural functionalism, conformity is a mechanism that helps maintain social order.[22] Members from minority groups may conform to established political norms as a means of securing stability and cohesion within a larger social system—even when that system exhibits authoritarian characteristics. This perspective, however, may obscure how conformity also reinforces existing inequities.

Coercive and Fear-Based Models

Finally, coercive and fear-based models argue that authoritarian regimes often enforce conformity through repression or the threat of violence.[23] Members of minoritized populations, frequently targets of such coercion, may adopt the dominant political narrative not out of ideological alignment but as a survival strategy, creating a façade of consensus that conceals underlying dissent.

---

21. Festinger, *Theory of Cognitive Dissonance*, 2–9.
22. Durkheim, *Division of Labor in Society*, 60–64.
23. Paxton, *Anatomy of Fascism*, 1–20.

Religious Frameworks for Understanding Political Conformity

The Case of Christian Nationalism

In addition to these sociocultural dynamics, religious ideologies have increasingly influenced political conformity in the United States. Christian nationalism—the belief that the nation is inherently and uniquely defined by Christian values—exerts strong normative pressure on religious communities. Kevin M. Kruse's *One Nation Under God: How Corporate America Invented Christian America* documents how corporate and political forces helped forge a national identity imbued with Christian symbolism, thereby reinforcing conformity among many USAmericans.[24]

"The Army of God Comes Out of the Shadows," by Stephanie McCrummen, offers a provocative and immersive portrait of the New Apostolic Reformation as a force reshaping USAmerican political and religious life. McCrummen vividly documents a fervent gathering at Gateway House of Prayer in Lancaster County, Pennsylvania, where apocalyptic imagery and militant rhetoric intertwine with the resurgence of Trumpism, suggesting that this charismatic movement is not merely a fringe phenomenon but increasingly emblematic of a broader, anti-democratic (or neo-democratic) trend. While her narrative is richly detailed and emotionally charged, it occasionally veers toward sensationalism, potentially obscuring the complex sociopolitical dynamics underlying the movement's appeal. Nonetheless, the article successfully challenges conventional understandings of USAmerican Christianity and democracy, urging readers to critically examine the unsettling convergence of religious zeal and authoritarian populism in today's political landscape.[25]

---

24. Kruse, *One Nation Under God*.
25. McCrummen, "Army of God."

The Case of Christian Zionism

Similarly, the phenomenon of Christian Zionism—which frames US and ultra-conservative global evangelicalism support for Middle Eastern policies in biblical terms—has contributed to a political environment in which alignment with dominant geopolitical narratives is seen as both a religious duty and a marker of national loyalty. For example, Stephen Spector's *Evangelicals and Israel: The Story of American Christian Zionism* (2009) examines how such beliefs have mobilized segments of the evangelical community to support specific foreign policies.[26] Although less extensively studied than Christian nationalism, Christian Zionism remains a significant factor in the mobilization of political conformity among certain groups.

In the same breath, Nicolas Panotto's clever article "Christian Zionism as Geopolitics and Public Theology: A Latin American Perspective" presents a provocative and comprehensive analysis of how Christian Zionist discourses have been mobilized as a tool for political conformity, particularly within Latin American conservative movements. Panotto adeptly traces the transformation of theological symbols—such as the flag of Israel—into powerful political signifiers that not only challenge secular liberal norms but also serve to legitimize policies aligned with a counter-hegemonic, imperial logic. His work illuminates the complex interplay between religious narratives and geopolitics, conflating symbolic rhetoric with direct policy impacts. Ultimately, the article effectively highlights the colonial dimensions of contemporary Christian Zionism and its power to reshape political identity, and a further discussion of its methodological nuances and generalizations could offer additional insights into its implications for democratic governance.[27]

---

26. Spector, *Evangelicals and Israel*.
27. Panotto, "Christian Zionism."

Implications for Minoritized Populations in the United States and Canada

The application of these frameworks becomes particularly illuminating when examining the political behavior of minority groups in the United States and Canada—nations that, despite their democratic credentials, have experienced episodes of authoritarian practices and political polarization.

During periods of social tension, minority communities have often employed divergent strategies of conformity and resistance. For instance, during the US civil rights movement, African Americans navigated a complex political terrain where overt conformity to dominant white political structures sometimes granted access to critical economic and social resources, while simultaneous acts of resistance challenged systemic injustice.[28] Similarly, in Quebec's Quiet Revolution, minority populations negotiated political conformity as a means of securing cultural recognition and stability, even as they challenged deep-seated inequalities.[29] In both cases, the decision to conform was shaped by pragmatic survival strategies as well as ideological negotiation—a dynamic that has increasingly come to be mediated by religious narratives.

In contemporary settings, minority groups in the United States and Canada face a dilemma: conform to dominant political narratives, which now often carry religious overtones, or resist in pursuit of long-term social justice. Modern voting patterns and party affiliations suggest that many minoritized voters opt for mainstream parties promising representation and material benefits. This pragmatic conformity is intertwined with religious identity; Christian nationalist rhetoric, for example, reinforces the idea that loyalty to the nation is inseparable from adherence to a particular set of religious values. Moreover, informational social influence—amplified by media echo chambers—further reinforces

---

28. Bobo and Gilliam Jr., "Race, Sociopolitical Participation, and Black Empowerment."

29. Maclure, *Quebec Identity*, 37–60.

the appeal of dominant, religiously infused narratives, offering both political and existential certainty.

Critical Reflections

Analyzing political conformity under authoritarian populist conditions highlights several tensions:

- Agency vs. Alignment: While normative social influence and social identity theory explain why minority groups might embrace dominant power structures, these same groups also exhibit forms of agency by negotiating—and sometimes subverting—the narratives surrounding them.[30]
- Cost-Benefit Limitations: Rational choice analyses can illuminate pragmatic benefits but risk reducing complex sociopolitical dynamics to a narrow economic logic. Religious and cultural identities add layers that shape decisions beyond mere utility.[31]
- Coercion vs. Normalization: Coercive models rightly emphasize the threat of violence or suppression, yet the steady normalization of repressive policies through religious or national narratives can be just as potent in shaping conformity.[32]
- Function vs. Inequity: Structural functionalism reminds us that conformity can promote social stability, but it may also perpetuate systemic inequities that drive further authoritarian tendencies.

Ultimately, understanding how and why these minoritized communities align—or dissent—reveals broader patterns at work in contemporary authoritarian populism. Recognizing the interplay of sociocultural dynamics, religious ideologies, and pragmatic

---

30. Tarrow, *Power in Movement*, 6–15, 160–65.
31. Tarrow, *Power in Movement*, 6–15, 142–45.
32. Skocpol, *States and Social Revolutions*.

survival strategies underscores the multifaceted and intersectional nature of political conformity.

Conclusion

Political conformity under authoritarian populism, as this chapter has shown, involves an intricate matrix of social, psychological, economic, and religious influences. From Trump-type fascism in the United States to systemic patterns of neoliberal governance throughout the American continent and the world, Western democracy faces a "regression" driven by antisocial capitalism, heightened surveillance, and racialized or religiously justified forms of exclusion.

The frameworks of normative and informational social influence, social identity theory, rational choice theory, cognitive dissonance, structural functionalism, and coercive models shed light on different dimensions of why individuals—especially from minoritized groups—conform in such environments. Meanwhile, Christian nationalism and Christian Zionism illustrate how religious narratives can intensify or legitimize authoritarian power structures in the backdrop of white normativity. By examining how these forces converge in contexts such as the United States and the American continent and at large, it becomes clear that *genuine* (participatory) democracy requires not only robust legal protections and cognitive justice, but also vigilant civic engagement informed by theological competence in order to resists manipulative political agendas.

In closing, if there is a single lesson to be gleaned from these overlapping pressures, it is that liberal/representative democracy is not only in regression but has failed because it is occupied by political and religious ideologies leading to authoritarian populism. At this point in history, we are no longer talking about "recovering" democracy but "democratizing democracy," to quote Boaventura de Sousa Santos.[33] Although the hegemonic model of

---

33. Santos, *Democratizing Democracy*, ixii–ixiii.

decaying democracy prevails worldwide, more recently, participatory democracy has gained renewed momentum, driven largely by subaltern communities and social groups resisting social exclusion and the erosion of full citizenship rights.

We have reached a point in history that survival of the Earth and humanity, God's creatures carrying the *imago Dei*, rests on continually confronting and questioning the processes by which political conformity is cultivated and naturalized. The distributed base movements in the world are beginning to realize their shared colonial oppressions, learning to organize in multifaceted ways, establishing glocal connections, and migrating from *conforming* to *co[i]nspiring*. Sooner or later a cataclysmic social change will take us by surprise by hoping societies embracing and emanating fear of injustice and upholding the rights and dignities of all citizens, especially those most vulnerable to authoritarian abuses. This is a theme for our next chapters.

Discussion Questions

For Community Organizers

- *Faith Motivations and Political Engagement*: Chapter 3 underscores how religious narratives, especially Christian ones, can both challenge and reinforce authoritarianism. As an activist, how do you ensure your faith-based actions remain genuinely prophetic rather than co-opted by partisan agendas? What spiritual practices or theological teachings sustain your commitment to democratic ideals and social justice?

- *Recognizing and Countering Authoritarian Tactics*: The chapter identifies tactics like polarizing discourse, denying unfavorable election results, and constructing "fake news." How might Christian activists effectively counter each of these in their advocacy work?

- *Empowering Minoritized Voices*: The text highlights that minoritized populations often face pressure to conform for survival. As an activist, how can you center and amplify these voices in ways that foster collective empowerment rather than token inclusion? In what concrete ways might you practice solidarity with marginalized communities to break cycles of fear-based conformity?

- *Addressing Internalized Ideologies:* Christian nationalism or Christian Zionism can become deeply rooted within faith communities. How do you engage believers who sincerely hold these ideologies but may be unaware of their authoritarian implications?

- *Building Participatory Democracy:* The chapter concludes with a call to "democratize democracy," suggesting that standard "liberal democracy" is failing. How do you see your role in forging more participatory and equitable models of social engagement within and beyond the religious institution? What forms of public theology or community organizing most effectively challenge the "regression of Western democracy" the chapter describes?

For Faith-Based Leaders

- *Spiritual Responsibility and Public Theology:* The chapter critiques "Trump-type fascism" as a manifestation of authoritarian populism. How do you see ministers being called to address or resist such manifestations from a faith perspective? In what ways can pastoral leadership help congregations critically evaluate political messages that appeal to Christian identity?

- *Conformity in Christian Communities:* Reflect on the role of Christian nationalism in shaping political conformity. What pastoral strategies could encourage congregants to discern between genuine faith commitments and partisan exploitation of religion?

- *Pastoral Care for the Marginalized:* The chapter highlights how minority groups sometimes adopt dominant political narratives for survival. How can ministers offer a space where marginalized believers feel safe expressing doubts or dissenting views? What biblical or theological resources could foster solidarity and hope rather than resignation in the face of authoritarian trends?

- *Prophetic Witness vs. Political Alignment:* In your pastoral experience, have you seen examples where speaking out against authoritarian tendencies strengthened or fractured community relationships?

- *Global Church Perspective:* Given that Christian congregations in many parts of the world face similar challenges (e.g., Brazil, Turkey, India), what can the global churches learn from each other about navigating authoritarian populist pressures? How might ecumenical or interfaith partnerships serve as a form of resistance to authoritarian impulses?

For the Classroom

- *Authoritarian Populism:* How does chapter 3 characterize "authoritarian populism," and in what ways do you see these traits manifest in contemporary political contexts?

- *Mechanisms of Conformity:* The chapter presents several frameworks (e.g., normative/informational social influence, social identity theory). Which framework resonates most with how you have observed people conforming to political or social norms in your community or online spaces?

- *Religion and Politics:* In your view, is it possible for religious convictions to positively influence democracy, or do they inherently risk fueling authoritarian tendencies?

- *Critical Thinking and Agency:* What practical steps could students take to remain informed and critical, preventing unreflective political alignment?

- *Global Perspectives:* How might studying these parallels help students develop a more nuanced understanding of global politics?

Chapter 4

From Conforming to Co(i)nspiring
—Toward a Post-Abyssal Imagination—

"Oh yes! Oh yes! Oh yes! All you people of Christ that are here oppressed, Imprisoned and scurrilously derided, gather yourselves together, you Wives and little ones, and answer to your several Names as you shall be shipped for his service, in the Westerne World, and more especially for planting the united Collonies of new England. . . . Know this is the place where the Lord will create a new Heaven and a new Earth in new Churches, and a new Common-wealth together."
—Edward Johnson (1628–1651)[1]

IT IS ALMOST FUNNY to read these early vision statements—the migration narratives that underwrite the foundational stages of the republic of the United States. I say "almost funny" because parallel biblical myths thread through both the Latino/a immigrant evangelical imagination and the so-called founding Christian pilgrim fathers of USAmerica. *The American Adam* of R. W. B. Lewis

---

1. Johnson, *Wonder-Working Providence*, 24–25, quoted in Benne and Hefner, *Defining America*, 5.

reemerges in the primal mythos of Whitman, Emerson, Thoreau, and the constitutional imaginations of Jefferson, Washington, and Franklin.[2] The Abrahamic and Mosaic myths, recodified into the "New Israel" of the Americas, are as undeniable as the present-day fact that "the people of America [today] can reenact their story without reference to the [ancient] people of Israel." Globally, the United States may be seen as the strongest political ally of the modern state of Israel, but our metaphorical dependence on the Abrahamic-Mosaic biblical arc remains unquestionable—even if we refuse to consciously acknowledge it.

Interestingly enough, my first pastor in the US was a Brazilian missionary sent from his homeland to "America" to evangelize immigrant Latinos/as believed to be sent by God to this country under the same divine mandate voiced in Johnson's claim: "for planting churches" that would awaken USAmerica to Christ. In fact, the completion of the evangelistic dreams of the original European pilgrims—fulfilled by today's recent pilgrims from the Global South—is precisely the claim made by a book written by an old friend, now with the Lord, *En la Tierra de los Peregrinos: La Iglesia Evangélica Hispana y Su Llamado Redentor*.[3] Like something out of a political satire, the largest immigrant populations supporting the Trump administration—anchored in the founding biblical myth of USAmerica—are the very ones most targeted by its anti-immigration laws. But satire, by nature, is a flipping story. It rarely conforms to a single narrative.

Chapter 3 reveals that political conformity under authoritarian populism is sustained by a complex interplay of social, psychological, economic, and religious forces: from Trump-style fascism in the United States to neoliberal patterns of governance across the Americas and beyond, Western democracy is regressing under antisocial capitalism, intensified surveillance, and racialized or religiously sanctioned exclusion. Theories of normative and informational influence, social identity, rational choice, cognitive dissonance, structural functionalism, and coercion illuminate why

2. Benne and Hefner, *Defining America*, 2–5.
3. Miranda, *En La Tierra de Los Peregrinos*.

people—especially those in minoritized communities—submit to such pressures. At the same time, Christian nationalism and Christian Zionism show how religious narratives can magnify and legitimize authoritarian structures within a framework of white normativity. Recognizing how these dynamics converge underscores that genuine participatory democracy depends not only on strong legal safeguards and cognitive justice but also on vigilant civic engagement informed by robust theological competence capable of resisting manipulative political agendas.

If there is a single lesson to be gleaned from these overlapping pressures, we said in the conclusion of chapter 3, it is that liberal (representative) democracy is not only in regression but has failed because it is now occupied by "extractive-immoral capitalism" and patriotic narratives leading to authoritarian (fascist) populism. In cases like the United States of America over the last ten years, the "environmentalism of the rich" has taken control of the state, the private sector, and the conservative religious sphere. The "fetishization of infinite growth and individual consumerism" as an expression of Christian nationalism and exceptionalism is more evident now than ever, quickly becoming the status quo across Western political economies.[4]

On the matter of "extractive-immoral capitalism," throughout this book, the reader will encounter expressions such as "extractive," "depredatory," and "immoral" capitalism. The central argument I put forward is that capitalism has evolved from a colonial economic experiment—dating back to the sixteenth century—into a global form of political-religious ideology. Both theological and non-theological voices engage with this perspective from various angles. For instance, Kathryn Tanner (*Christianity and the New Spirit of Capitalism*, 2019) and Joerg Rieger (*Theology in the Capitalocene*, 2022) recognize the profound spiritual and moral crises generated by capitalism as a global system. Enrique Dussel (*Ethics of Liberation in the Age of Globalization and Exclusion*, 2013) and Boaventura de Sousa Santos (*Epistemologies of the South*, 2014)

---

4. Santos, "Democracy in Dispute."

critique capitalism as both a product and perpetuator of colonial, epistemic, and ecological violence.

However, I consider Walter Mignolo's framework—the *Colonial Matrix of Power*—the most comprehensive approach for understanding and reimagining life at the borders of global capitalism (see, for instance, *The Politics of Decolonial Investigation*, 2021, Part III). Collectively, these scholars would agree that capitalism is neither neutral nor fundamentally virtuous. I align with Mignolo's view that extractive capitalism is grounded in systems of colonial domination that extend beyond the economic sphere—into culture, knowledge, gender, and ontology. Arguably, global capitalism promotes the idea of progress and prosperity on the basis of political conformity, in the backdrop of occupied democracy. Theologically speaking, then, capitalism as it truly exists—economically exploitative, ontologically depraving, ecologically extractive—is incompatible with the gospel's principles of shalom, jubilee, justice, liberation, and conviviality.

At this point in history—given the fact that global capitalism has occupied Western democracies—we should not be talking about "recovering" democracy but "democratizing democracy" (to quote Boaventura de Sousa Santos) as a movement forward to *re-form* the state and the global idea of citizenship.[5] Although the hegemonic model of decaying democracy prevails worldwide, participatory democracy has more recently gained renewed momentum, driven largely by subaltern communities and social groups resisting social exclusion and the erosion of full citizenship rights.

In this chapter, we will consider how to imagine a path leading away from political conformity and toward co(i)nspiring for a new social vision *rooted* in the unfolding kingdom of God as a countercultural alternative to the environmentalism of the rich and *privileged*—an occupied Christian democracy maintained by agents and structures sanctified by the fabricated God of the Matrix of Colonial Power. By con(i)nspiring, I mean an ecology of political reciprocity (interpolitics) and a theological praxis *delinked*

---

5. Santos, *Democratizing Democracy*, ixii–ixiii.

from the colonial fictions of extractive capitalism, patriarchy, and religious exceptionalism.

The first part of this chapter is devoted to understanding Santos's concept of the abyssal line as the place of marginality, erasure, and commodification of the majority of the population, with special attention to the poor, the immigrant, and minoritized populations in the Global North. The second part will venture into moving from political conformity to political co(i)nspiring as a theological experiment with two initiatives: (1) Christian views of democratizing democracy in correspondence to citizenship and the state, and (2) de-caricaturizing God, the land, and the Christian church. We hope to promote an ecology where another world and church are possible against the backdrop of indomitable political oppression and injustice.

The Rhetoric of Abyssal Thinking and Extractive-Immoral Capitalism

> What will happen when the natural resource boom comes to an end, and when it becomes evident that investment in natural resources was not properly offset by investment in human resources? What will happen when there is no money for generous compensation policies and sudden impoverishment creates a resentment difficult to manage in a democracy? When levels of environmental illnesses become unacceptable and overload public health systems to a point that makes them unsustainable? When water pollution, depletion of land and destruction of forests hits an irreversible point? When indigenous Afro-Brazilian Riparian and Quilombo peoples who were expelled from their land commit collective suicide or roam the urban peripheries claiming a right to the city that always will be denied to them?[6]

These concerns are not merely speculative—not for Boaventura de Sousa Santos and most of the Global South. Instead, they inform the concept of *abyssal thinking*, a framework that critiques

6. Santos, "Democracy in Dispute."

capitalism, colonialism, and patriarchy as forces that maintain global inequalities. Santos argues that modern Western thought creates an "abyssal line"—a conceptual boundary that separates those who are recognized as full citizens with human rights from those who are rendered invisible and dispensable.[7] This abyssal exclusion persists in economic, environmental, and epistemological domains, shaping how wealth, power, and knowledge are distributed globally. The so-called "natural resource" boom, often justified through capitalist development narratives, exacerbates these exclusions, reinforcing the systematic marginalization of Indigenous, Afro-Brazilian, and Quilombo communities, for instance.[8]

Historically, warnings about the environmental and social consequences of resource extraction have been dismissed as alarmist. This reflects a broader pattern within abyssal thinking, in which dominant political economies and media outlets maintain their legitimacy by marginalizing alternative perspectives.[9] Santos describes the global capitalist system as a "maelstrom" that prioritizes profit over human and ecological well-being. His call for an "anticapitalist ecological action" underscores the need to challenge the extractive model that treats nature and marginalized communities as disposable.[10]

The abyssal line, as articulated by Santos, is not merely a theoretical construct; it manifests in tangible ways, particularly in the governance of Earth's resources. Global trade policies, multinational corporations, and neoliberal development projects reinforce this division by ensuring that resource wealth benefits the elite while the environmental and social costs fall disproportionately on the poor.[11] The struggle over land and resources, particularly in Latin America, highlights how capitalism, colonialism,

---

7. Santos, *End of the Cognitive Empire*, 6–8.
8. Santos, *End of the Cognitive Empire*, 46.
9. Santos, *Epistemologies of the South*, 118–35.
10. Santos, "Democracy in Dispute"; Santos, *Epistemologies of the South*, 180–81.
11. Santos, "Toward an Aesthetics of the Epistemologies of the South."

and patriarchy work together to dispossess Indigenous and Afro-descendant communities.[12]

How does abyssal thinking work and what is its source? For Santos, modern Western thinking naturally generates abyssal thinking, which he describes as a system of visible and invisible distinctions that divide social reality into two realms. On one side of the abyssal line are visible and relevant people (the productive metropolitan class). Conversely, on the other side are people, cultures, and issues that become "invisible" and therefore irrelevant and "nonexistent."[13] In other words, people on the privileged, cosmopolitan side of the abyssal line experience the full benefits of citizenship and are considered worthy of human rights and dignity. On the other side of the abyssal line are the colonized, dispensable, non-metropolitan individuals who do not receive the full legal benefits of citizenship and whose needs, concerns, insights, and contributions receive little to no substantial attention from the political, economic, and educational systems.

Triple Pillars of Oppression

Santos asserts that capitalism, colonialism, and patriarchy are interwoven systems of domination.[14] The colonial legacy of land dispossession continues to define economic inequalities in the Global South, while patriarchal structures exacerbate gender-based exclusions from political and economic decision-making.[15] In Brazil, for example, Indigenous and Quilombo communities have faced systemic displacement due to agribusiness expansion, mining, and hydropower projects, all of which serve corporate interests at the expense of local populations.[16]

---

12. Santos, "Alternative to Utopia is Myopia."
13. Santos, "Beyond Abyssal Thinking."
14. Santos, "Epistemologies of the South and the Future."
15. Santos, "Postcolonialism, Decoloniality, and Epistemologies of the South."
16. Santos, "Resilience of Abyssal Exclusions in Our Societies."

From Conforming to Co(i)nspiring

Historically, the people living within Santos's abyssal line have been racial minorities, women, children, Indigenous people, the poor, and others marginalized by the colonial algorithm of human hierarchies described in chapter 1. Western colonization defined and globalized the abyssal line, but according to Santos, it is enforced, redefined, and perpetuated through capitalism, colonialism, and patriarchy. Within these triple pillars of oppression, people, histories, epistemologies, and forms of governance that do not come from, conform to, or affirm Western standards are rendered invisible, irrelevant, and nonexistent by cosmopolitan societies that turn a blind (or highly skeptical) eye and a deaf (or highly selective) ear to them.[17] Through this process of habitual, systemic dismissiveness, epistemicide and coloniality of knowledge are achieved.

Conformity, Epistemicide, and Post-Abyssal Imagination

One of the most insidious effects of abyssal thinking is epistemicide—the systematic devaluation of non-Western ways of knowing.[18] Like Santos, we have argued elsewhere that modern science and Western epistemology have historically dismissed Indigenous and Afro-descendant knowledge systems, labeling them as superstition or folklore.[19] This epistemic violence not only marginalizes alternative knowledge but also undermines resistance movements by depriving communities of their intellectual and cultural resources.

Pluralist epistemologies, according to Santos, recognize that all knowledge is context-dependent rather than absolute. He distinguishes this from relativism, which he critiques. Increased awareness, facilitated by access to and receptivity toward a plurality of epistemologies, creates greater opportunities for respectful dialogue, expanding intellectual growth and fostering connections

17. Santos, "Beyond Abyssal Thinking."
18. Santos, *Epistemologies of the South*, 92; Santos, "New Vision of Europe."
19. García-Johnson, *Spirit Outside the Gate*, 185–212.

between opposing perspectives. Santos asks, *"What is the connection that can create a bond of identity without fusion or messiness or lack of respect for the others?"*[20] For him, *"the process of intercultural translation is a movement from dispersion to bond.*[21] This movement is crucial because, according to Santos, induced conformity is upheld by capitalism, colonialism, and patriarchy—the three primary modes of domination in the West. These forces function collectively, yet resistance against them is often fragmented, rendering opposition efforts less effective.[22] Ultimately, greater connection and solidarity are necessary to enhance the viability of resistance strategies.

To transcend points of struggle, it is essential to identify the knowledge systems, social structures, and power-broking agendas that suppress communities along the abyssal line. Only then can new forms of knowledge, social structures, and agendas be discovered, developed, or improved. Pluralist epistemologies thrive in the shadowy borderlands of the abyssal line, where people are not empowered but rather oppressed by the intersecting forces of colonialism, patriarchy, and capitalism. Out of necessity, alternative knowledge systems and governance structures emerge or are reclaimed in these spaces. In short, the struggle to exist takes place at the abyssal line—but so does the will to resist. Thus, *aspiring allies must shed passivity by stepping away from centers of power to approach the abyssal line, investigate it, enter it, and learn to participate in the struggles that define it.* Active collaboration is essential for fostering connection, co(i)nspiration, and moving beyond the abyssal line.

To become collaborators, allies, and co(i)nspirers, if you will, we must also investigate ourselves. *We must be willing to discover how we are complicit or have been complicit in supporting systems of oppression* that render some people in our community's disposable through the colonial algorithm of human hierarchy that many of us have passively accepted. We have already discussed Santos's

---

20. Santos, "Politics of Translation," 14 min., 15 sec.
21. Santos, "Politics of Translation," 14 min., 15 sec.
22. Santos, "Politics of Translation," 5 min., 43–48 sec.

argument that learned ignorance and ignorant ignorance lay the groundwork for passivity to thrive in colonized spaces. Yet, philosopher Noam Chomsky and his colleague, Edward S. Herman, go so far as to claim that elite-guided mass media manipulation has been central to the functioning of capitalism in liberal democracies. According to these authors, the end goal of media manipulation has been to shape socio-historical narratives to manufacture political consent from citizens.

The Role of Media and Manufactured Consent

Santos's critique of abyssal thinking aligns well with Chomsky and Herman's theory of *manufactured consent,* which describes how mass media serves elite interests by shaping public discourse.[23] Chomsky and Herman argue that capitalist media structures filter information in ways that reinforce dominant ideologies, effectively silencing dissenting voices.[24] This process mirrors the epistemic exclusions described by Santos, as alternative narratives about capitalism, colonialism, and patriarchy are systematically delegitimized.

The media's role in maintaining abyssal thinking is particularly evident in its treatment of environmental justice movements. Activists who challenge extractive industries are frequently criminalized or dismissed as radicals, while corporate narratives of "sustainable development" dominate mainstream discourse.[25] By controlling which voices are amplified and which are silenced, media institutions perpetuate the abyssal line, ensuring that resistance remains fragmented and marginalized.[26]

---

23. Chomsky and Herman, *Manufacturing Consent,* lix–lxiv.
24. Chomsky and Herman, *Manufacturing Consent,* xi–xix.
25. Santos, "Politics of Translation."
26. Ndofirepi and Gwaravanda, "Boaventura de Sousa Santos' Epistemologies of the South."

Moving Beyond the Abyssal Line: Strategies for Resistance

To challenge the abyssal line, Santos calls for active engagement in struggles against capitalism, colonialism, and patriarchy.[27] This requires recognizing one's own complicity in systems of oppression and committing to epistemic justice. The recovery of Indigenous, Afro-descendant, and feminist knowledge traditions is central to this process, as these perspectives offer alternative frameworks for understanding and transforming society.

Santos emphasizes the need for "intercultural translation"—a practice of bridging diverse epistemologies without imposing a single universal standard. This process facilitates alliances between different resistance movements, allowing for more effective challenges to global systems of domination.[28] The struggle to move beyond the abyssal line, then, is not merely about critique but about the active construction of alternative futures.

Christian Ethics Outside the Gate: Theological Tricks for Post-Abyssal Resistance

The collapse of the extractivist economy in the Global North and South is not only ecological or economic—it is fundamentally ethical and theological, as we have argued. The cracks in global capitalism are revealing the fault lines of an abyssal world order that, as Santos claims, operates by rendering entire populations

---

27. This claim is central for Santos. He opens his book *The End of the Cognitive Empire* (Introduction) with a central claim that undergirds his entire decolonial project of cognitive justice. Santos envisions social mobilization as a force capable of dismantling and reforming the very structures produced by global capitalism, colonialism, and patriarchy. At the heart of Santos's contribution is the conviction that the oppressed must become agents of their own liberation and cognitive emancipation. Santos's vision and potential for public theology today is clearly captured in the 2024 article by the Spanish Liberation theologian Juan José Tamayo Acosta, "Decolonizing Knowledge: Boaventura de Sousa Santos' Vision."

28. Santos, "Toward an Aesthetics of the Epistemologies of the South, 117–25.

From Conforming to Co(i)nspiring

invisible beyond a line of epistemic and political exclusion.[29] The challenge is not merely to reform broken systems but to radically reimagine democracy, ethics, and the divine Self from the standpoint of the oppressed.

We venture next in a journey where Christian ethics engages decolonially in imaginative tasks: (1) democratizing democracy in correspondence to citizenship and the state, and (2) de-caricaturizing God, the land, and the Christian church. We hope to promote an ecology where another world and church are possible against the backdrop of indomitable political oppression and injustice. This is a theological experiment of imagining a world beyond the abyssal line.

Democratizing Democracy and the Covenant of Justice

Santos, like other decolonial theorists, critiques liberal representative democracy as a monocultural and exclusionary model rooted in colonial legacies.[30] He proposes *democratizing democracy* through what he terms *demodiversity*—a plural, participatory approach to politics that recognizes subaltern knowledges, community-based sovereignties, and intercultural legal systems.[31] Democracy in this view is not a static system but a dynamic project, constantly open to reinvention from below.

This vision finds theological resonance in Hak Joon Lee's covenantal framework for public theology and community organizing. In *God and Community Organizing*, Lee retrieves the Sinai covenant not as a private religious event, but as a communal political contract rooted in justice and accountability.[32] The covenant, for Lee, provides a relational foundation for democratic engagement, countering the atomized individualism of neoliberal democracy. Where Santos calls for pluralizing democratic agency, Lee grounds

---

29. Santos, *Reinventing Democracy*, 18–20.
30. Santos, *Reinventing Democracy*, 20–24.
31. Santos and Mendes, "Introduction," 1–28.
32. Lee, *God and Community Organizing*, 53–73.

that agency in the communal vocation of God's people—a vision that resonates strongly with grassroots justice movements in both religious and secular spheres.

Another distinguished Christian ethicist, Glen Stassen, likewise amplifies this approach by reclaiming the public significance of biblical justice. Drawing from the Beatitudes and prophetic texts, Stassen outlines four core dimensions of justice: deliverance of the poor, restraint of dominating power, pursuit of peace, and restoration of excluded persons.[33] In this framework, justice is not merely legal or moral—it is relational and communal, consistent with both Santos's emphasis on participatory structures and Lee's covenantal organizing.

All three thinkers resist what Santos critiques as the "abyssal logic" of Western political modernity, where the rights of the few are built on the invisibility of the many.[34] By emphasizing collective action, ethical community, and embodied justice, they provide a theological-political vision for reconstituting democracy as a space for liberation.

De-Caricaturizing God: The Politics of the Espíritu

In my volume two of the Nuevo Mundo Theology series (*Doctrina del Re-Conocimiento de Dios*, 2025, Editorial CLIE), I develop a section titled "The Doctrine of [De]Creation." This section examines the Western doctrine of creation with a focus on the human being and Mother Earth, articulated through ecological, theological, aesthetic, and ethical dimensions. I argue that the epistemic shifts brought about by the so-called "discovery of the New World" in the sixteenth century inaugurated a new mode of world-imagining for a select group of European powers. In a historically unprecedented move, local European kingdoms were transformed into global landlords, while Indigenous kingdoms and civilizations in Abya

---

33. Gushee and Stassen, *Kingdom Ethics*, 307–27.
34. Santos, *Reinventing Democracy*, 18–19.

From Conforming to Co(i)nspiring

Yala were reconstituted as landless populations and cheap global labor—what the text identifies as *colonial creations of empire*.

As a counter-narrative to these geo-theological *caricatures*, the human of the New World is reimagined as an eco-communitarian being, deeply interconnected with the Earth System (Mother Earth) and offered as an ontological alternative to the coloniality/modernity world system. The Western geopolitical/biopolitical reduction of bodies, places, and relationships to a colonial algorithm based on fourteen categories (see chapter 1) constitute the basis of extractive-immoral capitalism occupying liberal democracy nowadays—the very antithesis of God's kingdom of abundant life.

While democratizing democracy involves rethinking political structure, theology in the decolonial route must also confront distorted theological imaginaries. Santos notes how modern rights discourse, severed from deeper political-theological roots, can paradoxically reinforce neoliberal exclusion.[35] Similarly, Christian theology—especially in its colonial and Christendom iterations—has often functioned as a legitimating force for domination rather than liberation.

In my essay "Politics of the *Espíritu*," I directly address these concerns by calling for a pneumatological and decolonial reimagining of divine agency.[36] Doctrinally, I argue that Eurocentric Chalcedonian Christologies transplanted into the Americas have historically functioned to legitimize conquest, commodification of land, and the production of racialized hierarchies. In response, I propose a decolonial Spirit-ethics that disrupts these colonial logics by foregrounding the *Espíritu* as a liberative, relational, and insurgent presence among Indigenous, Black, and migrant communities. This Spirit-ethics operates within a framework of recognition–assemblage–decolonial healing, moving beyond abstract doctrinal formulations toward concrete practices of communal resistance and regeneration at the margins of empire.[37]

---

35. Santos, *If God Were a Human Rights Activist*, 45–62.
36. García-Johnson, "Politics of the *Espíritu*."
37. García-Johnson, "Politics of the *Espíritu*," 368.

Re-Cognition (Re-Conocimiento)

To understand the ethical framework it is necessary to elaborate on the epistemic economy of this concept. The concept of the *re-cognition* of God implies that God has been present, revealing and acting throughout the planet—before, through, and beyond human reasoning and language, hence, any civilizational imperial project. In this sense, our theory of divine knowledge affirms the Spirit of God as present, active, and compassionate within creation. This demands from creation a humble posture of openness to God—God's irresistible, omnipresent truth that regenerates the self-awareness of being (*metanoia*, a new mind) and dismantles the caricatures of our false identity and disfigured ways of living. The *re-cognition* of God, to borrow from the Indigenous imaginaries of the Global South in the Americas, is an inseparable *feeling-thinking* (*senti-pensar*).

The Spirit, or *Espíritu*, restores the *imago Dei* in communities deemed subhuman under coloniality/modernity civilizational projects. Where should a life-giving (probiotic) theological anthropology be grounded in colonial contexts? Certainly not in Westernizing Christology, which, as I have demonstrated, created theological orphanhood among Indigenous peoples by equating salvation with European cultural conformity.[38] A decolonial pneumatology resists this erasure by affirming the divine presence in native rituals, Afro–Latinx spirituality, and migrant survival practices.

Assemblage

The biblical narrative of Pentecost (Acts 2), in stark contrast to the biblical narrative of the Tower of Babel (Gen 11), begins at the epicenter of crisis—disorder, disorientation, and dissonant tongues—and ends in community, unity, and Spirit-empowered mission. Since the inception of the Christian church, these two narratives

---

38. García-Johnson, "Politics of the *Espíritu*"; Garcia-Johnson, *Spirit Outside the Gate*, 113–49.

have remained in perpetual tension: the imperial logic of Babel, building towers and borders to seize control of life, and the liberative logic of Pentecost, where the *Espíritu* disrupts oppressive conformity and assembles scattered peoples into dynamic, glocal communities of witness. While the imperial logic of Babel domesticates and subjects the vulnerable through homogenizing power, the insurgent logic of Pentecost reconfigures difference—not through erasure but through empowered dispersion—transforming disoriented laborers into Spirit-activated agents of kingdom life.

And yet, both logics have coexisted within the Western church as different colonial projects unfold around the world. This convergence demands critical questions. Are we, Westernized modern Christians, prepared for a Pentecost-shaped conviviality? Can we do ministry across tangled and plural cultural geographies? Can we operate beyond predictability, where the Spirit invites us into disruption and sacred perplexity? How do we embody collaboration with communities radically different from our own?

The *Espíritu* gathers dispersed and wounded identities not into uniformity but into *assemblages*—epistemic, ontological, geopolitical, and missional—formed through dance, protest, *abuelita* wisdom, song, and sacred land memory.[39] As I have observed, Indigenous theologies often arise outside academic canons, in spaces where the *Espíritu* political agency breathes life through embodied resistance.[40] These are not marginal practices of faith; they are Pentecost-based assemblages—lived intersections of power, knowledge, presence, and movement—challenging the empire's towers with the Spirit's glocal reworlding.

The *Espíritu* gathers dispersed and wounded identities into ethical communities of resistance. My work points to how Latinx and Indigenous theology often arises not in academic institutions but in *abuelita* wisdom, dance, song, protest, and the sacredness

---

39. García-Johnson, "Politics of the *Espíritu*," 367.
40. García-Johnson, *Spirit Outside the Gate*, 154–84.

of land.[41] These are not marginal expressions of faith—they are embodiments of the Spirit's political agency.

Decolonial Healing

Finally, the *Espíritu* heals not only individual wounds but communal disintegration. Drawing from theologians like George Tinker and Loida Martell-Otero, I have shown how Indigenous and Latina immigrant women have long participated in theological resistance through embodied Spirit-ethics.[42] Here the Spirit is not a doctrinal abstraction but a dancing, singing, wild force of transformation— "the wild child of the Trinity."[43]

This pneumatological ethics complements and extends Santos's call to democratize democracy: it decenters Eurocentric colonial fictions of divinity and opens space for *probiotic* theological geographies rooted in land, body, and communal re-existence.

From Conforming to Co(i)nspiring: The Theological Framework

Generating a language that inspires a new social imaginary is one of the tasks of doing theology in the public space. The voices we have included in this chapter reveal the possibility of a shared vision of political nonconformity and decolonial dissent oriented by Spirit-ethics. Grounded in communal struggle, participatory democracy, and decolonial pneumatology, this shared vision of nonconformity offers some concrete postures:

- Resisting extractive-immoral capitalism and patriarchal religion by rooting justice in covenantal solidarity and Spirit-assemblages.

---

41. García-Johnson, "Politics of the *Espíritu*," 367.

42. García-Johnson, "Politics of the *Espíritu*;" Tinker, *Spirit and Resistance*; Martell-Otero et al., *Latina Evangélicas*.

43. Martell-Otero et al., *Latina Evangélicas*, 20–31.

- Transforming human rights from metropolitan individual entitlements to collective liberation in the abyssal line.
- Reclaiming the divine not as imperial Sovereign fiction, but as liberating *Espíritu* present in marginalized geographies and living spaces.
- Practicing justice as embodied, daily solidarity with the poor, the displaced, and the disfigured.

It is a Spirit-ethics born *outside the gate*—not within the sanctuaries of power or the institutions of empire. The *Espíritu* is not waiting for Easter Sunday. She is already dancing in Holy Saturday, singing in occupied zip codes, building life amid death.[44]

This is the decolonial revolution of the *Espíritu*—one that reverses the social order, reclaims the dignity of the oppressed, reciprocates to Mother Earth, and anticipates a pluriversal future where all cultures and peoples have a place. This, indeed, is what we mean by democratizing democracy for the unfolding kingdom of God.

"God's Resistance" as Co[i]nspiring: Sacred Resistance Beyond Political Revolt

How do we recognize con[i]nspiring when we face it or perform it even? I have known *La Madrina*—the godmother—Rev. Dr. Alexia Salvatierra, for over a decade. That title, given to her during the early days of the sanctuary movement in the 1980s, is both affectionate and profoundly accurate. She is not only my friend and colleague but also my academic dean at Fuller Seminary. If anyone in our Southern California context embodies the gospel mandate "Behold, I am sending you out as sheep in the midst of wolves, so be wise as serpents and innocent as doves" (Matt 10:16, ESV), it is Salvatierra. Her life and praxis reflect a theology of holy defiance—an incarnational wisdom honed in protest, prayer, and pastoral solidarity. In many ways, the co-authored volume *God's*

---

44. García-Johnson, "Politics of the *Espíritu*," 368.

Resistance: Mobilizing Faith to Defend Immigrants (2023) serves as a lived articulation of that biblical mandate—offered as a grounded theory shaped by a team of diverse activist scholars.

Influenced by Salvatierra's vision and missiological depth and enriched by the expertise of two sociologists and a Chicano historian, *God's Resistance* advances a grounded theory of resistance that emerges directly from the lived experiences of faith-based organizing in Latina/o Christian communities. This theory shows how sacred narratives, spiritual practices, and community structures mobilize marginalized communities not merely to survive systemic injustice but to generate what our book calls *re-existence*—a theological and practical reassertion of humanity, agency, and sacred identity in defiance of dehumanizing systems. Put simply, the book unveils how communities expected to conform have instead found ways to co(i)nspire.

God's Resistance does not impose a theory from above but constructs one from below—through participatory research that includes extensive interviews, ethnographic observation, and deep engagement with immigrant-rights faith networks. This research illustrates how oppressed communities reframe doctrine into an instrument of agency: faith functions not only as moral compass but as an organizational scaffold. The result is a framework that resists exclusion through spiritual narrative, communal solidarity, and embodied advocacy. Ultimately, the authors present a sacred counter-world—a praxis of *re-existence*—that repudiates domination and reclaims divine-human dignity.

The book captures this sacred resistance through a matrix of operations—distinct yet overlapping, and often asynchronous—that shape how resistance is embodied:

1. *Faith as Dual Agency*: The authors present a nuanced view of faith as both constraint and catalyst. While Christian traditions provide theological energy for resistance (e.g., Jesus as a refugee, God's solidarity with the oppressed), they also

examine how Eurochristian dominance can discourage radical engagement through institutional conservatism.[45]

2. *Scripture as Political Catalyst*: Sacred texts such as Leviticus 19 and Matthew 25 are not abstract ideals but active warrants for public theology. Participants interpret them as divine imperatives to welcome the stranger, resist injustice, and enact Christlike solidarity.[46]

3. *Spiritual Capital as Community Wealth*: Building on Tara Yosso's model of community cultural wealth, the book identifies *spiritual capital*—the embodied resilience, moral courage, and oppositional imagination that faith produces—as a resource for activism, especially visible in rituals, testimonies, and intercessory prayer.[47]

4. *Faith-Based Organizations as Bridging Institutions*: Churches and religious networks function as "bridging" institutions—intermediaries connecting undocumented individuals with legal, housing, and emotional support that would otherwise be inaccessible.[48]

5. *Sacred Resistance Beyond Political Resistance*: Resistance here is not only about policy change; it is liturgical and existential. Drawing from liberation theology and base ecclesial communities, *God's Resistance* casts re-existence as a moral reorientation—toward beloved community and the inbreaking kingdom of God.[49]

6. *Multipronged Targeting: Theology, Policy, Culture*: The movement targets not only unjust immigration laws but also internalized oppression within immigrant communities

---

45. Christerson et al., *God's Resistance*, 141–48.
46. Christerson et al., *God's Resistance*, 129–31.
47. Christerson et al., *God's Resistance*, 134–36.
48. Christerson et al., *God's Resistance*, 133–34.
49. Christerson et al., *God's Resistance*, 144–48.

and cultural apathy in white Christian spaces—challenging single-issue paradigms with a holistic strategy.[50]

7. *Grassroots Agency in Marginalized Faith Communities:* Undocumented clergy and lay leaders are not passive recipients of advocacy but its protagonists. Through base communities and trauma-informed pastoral models, they enact a participatory epistemology in which faith and lived experience generate knowledge and movement.[51]

In short, these interwoven practices reveal a sacred insurgency that transcends the binaries of reform versus revolution. Rather than merely leaning left or right, *God's Resistance* invites us into what I call co(i)nspiring—a theological reframe where resistance is not just against oppression but *toward* a Spirit-breathed reimagining of what it means to be human together.

Discussion Questions

For Community Organizers

- *Locating the "Abyssal Line" in Our Zip Code:* Where, concretely, do you see people rendered invisible or "disposable" in your city? What everyday practices (permits, policing, zoning, language, media) keep that line in place?
- *From Extractive to Generative Economics:* If extractive-immoral capitalism is the air we breathe, what small-scale economic experiments (co-ops, time banks, land trusts, reparations funds) could crack it open where you live?
- *Manufactured Consent and Local Media:* Which local news outlets or social media feeds shape public opinion in ways that reinforce passivity? How might organizers create counter-narratives that center marginalized voices?

---

50. Christerson et al., *God's Resistance*, 143–48.
51. Christerson et al., *God's Resistance*, 68–92.

From Conforming to Co(i)nspiring

- *Plural information in the Streets:* How can Indigenous, Afro-descendant, immigrant, or disabled knowledge systems guide the tactics and rhythms of your campaigns—beyond symbolic inclusion?

- *Co(i)nspiring Across Movements:* What would real reciprocity look like between housing justice, ecological defense, and racial-gender liberation groups in your region? Where are the friction points—and how might Spirit-led "assemblage" help?

- *Metrics of Liberation:* Traditional campaigns measure wins in policy changes. What alternative indicators (well-being, land returned, languages revived, police encounters reduced) would signal that we are democratizing democracy from below?

- *Animating God's Resistance on the Block: God's Resistance* shows immigrant congregations converting spiritual capital—rituals, testimonies, intercessory prayer—into organizing power that defends the undocumented and approximates "re-existence." What parallel practices could your tenant union, mutual-aid network, or coalition translate into its own context so that resistance is not only political but sacred, story-driven, and communal?

For Faith-Based Leaders

- *Decolonizing our Theological Imagination:* Where do sermons, liturgies, or curricula still mirror "imperial Sovereign" images of God that bless extractive capitalism? What might a Spirit-ethics of *conviviality* sound like on Sunday?

- *Covenantal Justice and Church Budgets:* Hak Joon Lee links covenant to public accountability. How do your budget lines (building maintenance, salaries, missions, endowment investments) reveal or betray covenantal priorities?

- *Pentecost versus Babel in Congregational Life:* In what ways does your faith community unintentionally enforce Babel-like homogeneity (language, style, politics)? What practices could welcome Pentecost's "sacred perplexity" instead?

- *Spiritual Formation for Political Non-Conformity*: What rhythms of prayer, study, or pilgrimage would equip congregants to resist manufactured consent and ethno-nationalism?

- *Eco-Theology in the Age of "Environmentalism of the Rich"*: How can preaching and sacramental life expose greenwashing while nurturing concrete ecological reparations (e.g., church-land agro-forestry, carbon fasting tied to jubilee economics)?

- *Confession of Complicity*: Design a liturgical act that helps worshippers name personal and institutional complicity in the "triple pillars" (capitalism, colonialism, patriarchy) without lapsing into paralyzing guilt.

- *Liturgizing Sacred Co-(i)nspiring: God's Resistance* depicts worship spaces where Scripture (e.g., Lev 19; Matt 25) becomes a warrant for public sanctuary, and where "holy defiance" is rehearsed in prayers, testimonies, and lament. Design one congregational practice—a vigil, Eucharist, or children's lesson—that would let your faith community *rehearse* that kind of "holy defiance" as covenantal discipleship every week.

For the Classroom

- *Theory Synergy*: Compare Santos's "abyssal line" with Chomsky and Herman's "manufactured consent." Where do the frameworks reinforce each other, and where do they diverge in diagnosing power?

- *Case-Study Autopsy*: Choose a recent example of resource extraction (e.g., lithium in the Atacama, Line 3 in Minnesota). Map the actors on both sides of the abyssal line and identify the media filters at work.

From Conforming to Co(i)nspiring

- *Grounded-Theory Studio: Mapping God's Resistance:* Analyze one chapter or field vignette from *God's Resistance: Mobilizing Faith to Defend Immigrants.* (a) name the emergent concepts in the authors' grounded theory (spiritual capital, sacred counter-world, re-existence, etc.); (b) diagram how those concepts operationalize Santos's "democratizing democracy"; and (c) test how transferable that framework is to another struggle (climate migration, prison abolition).

- *Debate: Democratizing Democracy:* Stage a structured debate: "Resolved: Liberal representative democracy can be repaired from within." Require students to marshal evidence from Boaventura de Sousa Santos and Hak Joon Lee.

- *Epistemicide and Curriculum Design:* Audit your syllabus. Which voices remain invisible? How might "intercultural translation" reshape the learning objectives and assessment methods of this course?

- *Theology in the Capitalocene—Thought Experiment:* Ask students to imagine a worship service set in 2050 after a partial collapse of extractivist economies. What liturgical symbols survive? What new rituals emerge?

- *Embodied Research Methods:* Inspired by the chapter's emphasis on "senti-pensar," have students conduct a day of fieldwork using sensory ethnography (sound mapping, soil touching, participatory photography) to encounter lived experiences along an abyssal line in their own city.

- *From Conforming to Co(i)nspiring—Personal Reflection:* Write a reflective essay tracing one place in your life where you "conform to the matrix" and one concrete step you will take to co(i)nspire a different social vision this term.

Chapter 5

Cracking Babel!
—Pentecost Re-Existencia in the Era of Imperial Populism—

For those who stubbornly seek freedom, there can be no more urgent task than to come to understand the mechanisms and practices of indoctrination. These are easy to perceive in the totalitarian societies, much less so in the system of "brain-washing under freedom" to which we are subjected and which all too often we serve as willing or unwitting instruments.[1]

THE TRUMPET'S ECHO OF *AMERICA First* reverberated through rust-belt arenas and spiraled up gleaming towers like a twenty-first-century reprise of Shinar.[2] The architecture was familiar: a single tongue of grievance, a single dream of restored greatness, a single fear of scattering. In other words—Babel rebooted.[3] Yet even as border walls were promised and travel bans drafted, another wind was rising from below. It carried the scent of tortillas and kimchi, the cadence of Mapudungun laments, the laughter of DACA-mented college sophomores, and the prophetic cackle of

---

1. Chomsky, "Manufacture of Consent," 136.
2. Mudde, *Far Right Today*, 1–25.
3. García-Johnson, *Spirit Outside the Gate*, 232–35; 252–53.

Abuelita María, who has survived five presidents and is not about to flinch for this one. That wind is the Spirit's counter-plot in the Trump era, summoning the church to what Latin American Indigenous communities call *re-existencia*—the decision to inhabit the world otherwise while empire still patrols the streets.[4]

Babel Redux: Authoritarian Populism as Theopolitical Fear Management

Authoritarian populism thrives by weaponizing what Walter Brueggemann names "the fortress mentality"[5]—an anxiety that sacrifices diversity on the altar of monoculture and labels such sacrifice "security." Political scientists Cas Mudde and Cristóbal Rovira Kaltwasser trace the present variant to a global wave (Hungary, India, Israel, Argentina, El Salvador, Russia, Venezuela, the United States) wherein charismatic leaders claim exclusive representation of "the real people" against allegedly parasitic elites and threatening outsiders.[6] As we have shown in previous chapters, authoritarian populism has become a political theology of fear and conformity: a promise of salvation through uniform language, sealed borders, insane international tariffs, transnational concentration camps (jails), and golden age nostalgic myths.

Theologically, this posture mirrors Genesis 11: the builders' dread of being "scattered abroad upon the face of the whole earth" (Gen 11:4). Their tower is less an act of architectural genius than a monument to anxiety—"oppressive conformity."[7] Empire's genius is to transmute that anxiety into policy: citizenship tests, voter ID laws, family separations, algorithmic surveillance, mass deportation, and incarceration of "the wretched" of the land. In each, there lurks a Babel logic: *Make it one, or make it disappear.*

---

4. Hurtado and Porto-Gonçalves, "Resistir y Re-existir."
5. Brueggemann, *Genesis*, 116–18.
6. Mudde and Kaltwasser, *Populism*, 24–41.
7. García-Johnson, *Spirit Outside the Gate*, 238–47; 255.

Pentecost as Decolonial Scatter

What would it take to join God in the scattering of the Babel project? Acts 2 narrates God's unruly reply. The Spirit does not erase Babel's scattering—she transcends it, converting dispersion into polyphonic communion where "each one heard them speaking in the native language of each" (Acts 2:6). I insist we read Pentecost "not as a reversal but as a forward achievement," a glimpse of an order Babel could never imagine—pluriversal, glocal, vernacular, multivocal, public.[8]

Decolonial thinkers of Abya Yala name that forward achievement *re-existencia*. Carlos Walter Porto-Gonçalves first heard the term among Amazonian *seringueiros* who defended forest and culture simultaneously;[9] Catherine Walsh braided it into a pedagogy of "resisting, (re)existing, and (re)living."[10] *Re-existence is sabotage by flourishing*: scatter, sing your own tongue, plant milpa in the shadow of the plantation, livestream Mass in Spanglish from a detention center parking lot. It refuses empire's ultimatum—assimilate or vanish—and responds instead with Pentecost improvisation: *We scatter, therefore we live*. Migration, disguise, transnationality, outernationality, borderlines, liminality, hybridity, cosmopolitanism, *Nepantla*.

Fear as Fertile Ground

The paradox of our moment is that the very fear authoritarianism manipulates can become soil for gospel generativity. In *Spirit Outside the Gate* I argued that God's disruptive scattering in Babel "anticipates a much more advanced cultural and missional project" than human monoculture.[11] The Trump era merely intensifies the conditions for that anticipation. When Muslim neighbors are vilified, churches practicing *iftar* hospitality taste Pentecost fire.

---

8. García-Johnson, *Spirit Outside the Gate*, 236–37.
9. Hurtado and Porto-Gonçalves, "Resistir y Re-existir."
10. Walsh, "Introducción."
11. García-Johnson, *Spirit Outside the Gate*, 234.

Cracking Babel!

When ICE raids sow dread, congregations that turn fellowship halls into sanctuaries inhale Spirit-breath. Fear, inverted by grace, becomes fuel for imaginations otherwise anesthetized by privilege.

Four Conversions for a Church Without Borders

What, then, does *re-existence* require of an ecclesia formed in Trump-era turbulence?

- *From Monolingual Pulpits to Polyglot Liturgies*
  Pentecost authorizes every tongue as a theological instrument. Preaching that rotates between English, K'iche', and Korean without apologizing signals that no language owns revelation. Translation is still offered—but as mutual intelligibility and hospitality, not hierarchy and cognitive control.

- *From Fortress Community to Intercultural Scatter*
  Safety cannot be the church's organizing principle. Congregations must embrace what Willie Jennings imagines as a *reconfigured (reversed) place of belonging and intimacy*[12]— planting worship gatherings in laundromats, partnering with mosques for disaster relief, risking government scrutiny by protecting immigrants.

- *From Apartheid Missions to Glocal Partnership*
  Dominant-culture institutions must yield authority to diasporic and Indigenous leaders, not as token advisers but co-architects. Mission compacts should flow south-to-north/east-to-west as readily as north-to-south/west-to-east, reversing the colonial paternalism of twentieth-century Christendom.

- *From Amnesiac Patriotism to Prophetic Recordar (Memory)*
  Re-existence feeds on truthful recollection: broken treaties, redlined neighborhoods, internment camps. As in the post-Easter Lukan narrative of "On the Road to Emmaus" (Luke

12. Jennings, *Christian Imagination*, 288.

24), the Eucharist becomes an act of public remembering that refuses national myth. This act of remembering is a resurgent memory—that is, "the disconformity that recovers the possibility of not ratifying the gated present."[13]

From *God's Resistance* to *Re-Existir*

In the previous chapter, we introduced *God's Resistance* as a grounded theory that frames how some faith-based communities are embedding sacred stories as they resist oppression, hence, offering more than a political revolt and by so doing they approximate *re-existir*. Attempting a simplification, we could venture into the following diagram:

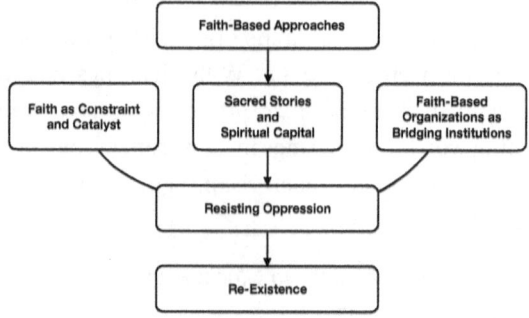

Grounded Theory for Resisting Oppression and Moving toward Re-Existence

---

13. García-Johnson, *Spirit Outside the Gate*, 232.

Cracking Babel!

Alignment Between God's Resistance and Ecclesial Praxis of Re-Existir

1. From Monolingual Pulpits to Polyglot Liturgies

Diagram Link: Sacred Stories and Spiritual Capital → Resisting Oppression

This liturgical transformation embodies spiritual capital in linguistic form-treating language diversity as sacred rather than problematic. The act of preaching in multiple languages is a resistance to monolingual ecclesial supremacy and a move toward *re-existence* through radical hospitality and epistemological humility. Pentecost becomes both theological event and organizing principle.

2. From Fortress Community to Intercultural Scatter

Diagram Link: Faith-Based Organizations as Bridging Institutions → Resisting Oppression → Re-Existence

This move reflects how faith communities shift from inward preservation to outward solidarity. The diagram's emphasis on *bridging institutions* is echoed here: planting churches in laundromats or collaborating with mosques enacts a tactical scattering that creates re-existence through unlikely coalitions and shared vulnerability.

3. From Apartheid Missions to Glocal Partnership

Diagram Link: Faith as Constraint and Catalyst → Resisting Oppression

The critique of white Christian paternalism is a prime example of *faith as constraint*. But our ecclesial proposal models the catalytic side—an ecclesiality that resists colonial theological imperialism and welcomes diasporic leadership. It rewrites power through glocal mission partnerships, embodying sacred resistance to empire while constructing new missional architectures.

4. From Amnesiac Patriotism to Prophetic Recordar (Memory)

Diagram Link: Spiritual Capital + Sacred Stories → Re-Existence

This is perhaps the deepest resonance with re-existence. Prophetic memory—the refusal to forget genocide, slavery, internment, land theft—activates sacred narrative as a site of resistance. Like the Emmaus story, remembrance becomes insurgent theology. Here, re-existence is both the fruit and the praxis of prophetic remembering.

In short, both approaches envision re-existence not merely as survival, but as transformation. The diagram offers a structural backbone, while the fourfold ecclesial transformations embody the dynamic movement of faith-in-action—particularly within communities disrupted by nationalism, racism, and global migration. What follows illustrates how re-existir continues to unfold not in lockstep, but with fluidity—without the straitjacket of fixed models. It compels us to act more like storm chasers than field marshals, pursuing unpredictable currents of Spirit-led transformation rather than attempting to manage or domesticate them.

Signs of Pentecost Re-Existir

1. Caracoles Zapatistas, Chiapas: Spiral Centers of Autonomy

Since 2003, the Zapatista movement has organized its autonomous governance through the *caracoles* (literally, "snails") and the *Juntas de Buen Gobierno* (Councils of Good Government). These structures embody the principle of *mandar obedeciendo*—to lead by obeying—and practice a radical form of self-governance that includes health clinics, autonomous schools, women's collectives, and Indigenous justice systems.[14]

In 2023, amid a sharp uptick in cartel-linked and paramilitary attacks on Indigenous communities, the Ejercito Zapatista de

---

14. Servicio Internacional para la Paz (SIPAZ), "Path of the Caracol Towards Autonomy."

Liberación Nacional (EZLN) reorganized internally and closed its caracoles to outside visitors to protect residents. This move suspended high-profile initiatives such as the Escuelita Zapatista, last held in 2013–2014, when thousands of international students learned agroecology, Indigenous jurisprudence, and autonomous governance in Chiapas. Like the insurgent movement of Jesus as registered in the book of Acts, the Zapatistas' educational outreach entered a security-driven pause, underscoring how autonomy must sometimes retreat in order to survive. These gatherings and self-contracting trajectories enact a Pentecost-communal imagination of multiple tongues and decentralized power, demonstrating that pluriversality can be administratively embodied, not just poetically invoked.[15]

The Zapatista caracoles are living testimony that re-existence is not reactionary nostalgia, but a forward-pointing construction of political, educational, and spiritual life against empire's monocultures.

2. Pueblo Kichwa de Sarayaku: The Living Forest Speaks

The Kichwa people of Sarayaku, Ecuador, situated deep in the Amazon, have made history by legally declaring their territory a *Kawsak Sacha*—a Living Forest endowed with its own spirit and agency. In 2012, after a landmark case at the Inter-American Court of Human Rights, Sarayaku secured recognition of their right to free, prior, and informed consent over extractive projects.

Building on this, between 2021–2023, Sarayaku leaders launched a *Plan de Vida* ("Plan of Life") that integrates solar microgrids, community-run schools emphasizing ecological spirituality, and ecotourism practices that align with the defense of the Living Forest. The Spirit of Pentecost—who breathed diverse tongues into the early church—breathes here as the trees themselves are named subjects of communal worship and guardianship.[16]

---

15. Santos Cid, "Mexico's Zapatistas Warn"; Clemente, "Mexico's Zapatista Rebel Movement"; "Zapatista School."

16. Corte Interamericana de Derechos Humanos, *Caso Pueblo Indígena*

Sarayaku's struggle is not merely resistance; it is a re-existence that redefines development through Amazonian cosmology and Mother Earth's rights.

3. Guardia Indígena del Cauca, Colombia: Unarmed (Pentecost-Shaped) Defenders

Founded in 2001 by the Indigenous peoples of Cauca, Colombia, the *Guardia Indígena* is a civil, unarmed resistance movement formed to defend their territories and lives amidst civil war, paramilitary violence, and drug cartels. Their defense tactics include *bastones de mando*—wooden staffs symbolizing communal authority—and collective patrols that embody a theology of protective solidarity.[17]

In early 2024, during some of Colombia's bloodiest armed clashes in years, the Guardia organized humanitarian corridors to safely escort more than 20,000 civilians. This act dramatizes Pentecost's logic: unarmed bodies, scattered but united, become witnesses against the forces of Babel.

Their resistance is not merely civic but theological: a public liturgy of life where every marcher, elder, and child declares, "You will not erase us." Their re-existence defies the state's failure and militarization with Spirit-empowered community autonomy.

4. Coharie Indigenous Resistance, Resilience, and Re-Existence in Rural North Carolina

In rural eastern North Carolina, small communities of Coharie Native American Indians cluster along the Black River and its tributary, the Great Coharie Creek. According to tribal lore, memory rides the wind along the water's bank where pine needles rustle overhead, echoing the sound of mothers of long ago, who hushed

---

Kichwa de Sarayaku vs. Ecuador; Pueblo Originario Kichwa de Sarayaku, *Kawsak Sacha*.

17. Consejo Regional Indígena del Cauca (CRIC), "La Guardia Indígena."

their children to shield them from approaching strangers.[18] The Coharie people's oral tradition also recalls Roanoke's "Lost Colony," of 1587, a migration from the Neuse, and centuries of hospitality—welcoming Europeans and the formerly enslaved into tribal life.[19] That openness later hurt them: bureaucrats demanded racial pedigrees, colonial records were sparse, and their language frayed.[20]

Yet the Coharie never vanished; they practiced re-existence, reshaping life on their own terms. Christianity, paradoxically, became a vessel of this re-existence despite being the faith of the colonizers. Though no record details the tribe's conversion, the faith does not seem to have been either imposed or passively accepted. It was adapted—rooted in brush arbors beneath trees named Faith, Hope, and Charity—into a communal architecture that sustained education, governance, and communal care by folding tribal life into churches born under the shade of those trees.[21] Today, the Coharie tribe openly credits their endurance to the Christian God and their collective will.[22] Churches remain the tribe's backbone. Through colonial invasion, revolution, Civil War, Jim Crow, and forced integration, they kept transforming rather than yielding.

State recognition finally came in 1971. Tribal administrator Greg Jacobs recalls feeling "like we were underground for so long . . . when the commission formed, the wall we hid behind came down."[23] With recognition came revived traditions, better schooling, jobs, and political access—hope then, hope still.

Today the Coharie have reclaimed their river. Fear has been inverted. Strangers are now invited to experience the nurturing peace of its gentle currents and sheltering trees. Along its banks, they still cultivate gardens that feed not only their own elders

---

18. Coharie Tribe, "History."

19. Grady, "Coharie Indians."

20. See Butler, *Croatan Indians of Sampson County, North Carolina*.

21. Berde, *Politics and Prayers*; Coharie Tribe, "History."

22. Berde, *Politics and Prayers*. Also, see Lignum Crucis Productions, *Our People*; and Coharie Tribe, "History."

23. Liggett, "Survivance."

and families, but anyone in need.[24] Their tribal center is a place of learning and reciprocity, where knowledge is shared and care is extended without condition. This ethic of hospitality stands as quiet defiance against centuries of imposed hierarchy and racialized control.

Under the long shadow of colonial domination and the bureaucratic authoritarianism of the postcolonial state, the Coharie have shrewdly met each challenge, refusing to give up on their values, customs, or tribal identity. In their churches—now alive with Pentecostal fervor—they practice a spirituality that is open, embodied, and rooted in collective memory. Drums and dancing are welcome. Prayers are fervent, and though their ancestral language is forgotten, they have welcomed the language of the Spirit. Indigenous rituals are making a comeback at weddings and funerals, and powwows are now echoing with both Native rhythms and Southern gospel harmonies. These are not contradictions, but convergences—acts of survival made sacred.

Visible and thriving, the Coharie embody re-existence—creative, communal, and free—daily defying the systems that once sought to contain them.

5. Babel Crackers: The Resurgence of Multilingual/Intercultural/Intergenerational/Transnational/Interpolitical Urban Ministries

It's breaking out, more often than not, over shared plates and sidewalk vigils. One day very soon, Korean bodegas will host Virgen-de-Guadalupe novenas, Salvadoran pastors will quote Minjung theology, and Spirit-teachings will cross-pollinate faster than ICE can knock. Every scene upends Babel's playbook—homogeneity, hierarchy, selective amnesia, racial capitalism—by riffing Pentecost's street-level jazz of solidarity and song.

In Los Angeles—the Azusa Street Revival's (1906) old neighborhood—still pulses with that groove but from a different place

---

24. Dunne, "Coharie Tribe."

Cracking Babel!

of enunciation: *glossolalia* as decolonizing *glocality*.[25] On a typical Sunday the Spirit slips off the I-10 at San Gabriel Boulevard and glides into Evergreen Baptist Church of Los Angeles, a congregation that began in 1925 as a Japanese-language mission in Boyle Heights and replanted itself in Rosemead in 1988 to follow its second- and third-generation members into the San Gabriel Valley. Beneath the cross-beamed ceiling, Nisei elders who remember Manzanar worship beside Chinese software engineers, Filipino nurses, Latino neighbors, and Korean art school students—a mosaic that now spans at least seventeen Asian ethnicities along with Black, Latino, and white Angelenos. Scripture is read in English, but prayers drift into Japanese or Tagalog, and on festival Sundays Kodama taiko drums shake the walls before the praise band settles into contemporary worship. When the benediction ends, the fellowship hall enacts the church's self-description as a "Home for the New Humanity of God": congregants linger over shared lunches, exchanging recipes, testimonies, and languages until afternoon light slants through the glass doors.[26]

The Spirit has a regular route through Boyle Heights: she slips under the ceaseless hum of the I-5, crosses Gless Street, and settles in the cool adobe hush of Dolores Mission Church, a Jesuit parish founded in 1925 to serve Spanish-speaking immigrants.[27] Inside, folding chairs share space with votive candles because pews alone cannot contain the restless hope of a neighborhood hemmed in by the Pico Gardens and Pueblo del Sol housing projects.[28] Ninety-plus percent of parishioners are Latino, and many live below the federal poverty line, yet every week they gather in *Comunidades Eclesiales de Base*—small "base communities" that read the day's Gospel, compare it with rent hikes or gang violence, and plot the

---

25. I treat these two concepts side by side in García-Johnson, *Mestizo/a Community of the Spirit*, 80–101.
26. Evergreen Baptist Church of Los Angeles, "About"; Kang, "Building on the Gospel of Inclusion"; Chuang, "Churches that Last for Generations."
27. Dolores Mission Church, "About."
28. Morrison, "Little Church of Immigrants."

next act of collective mercy.²⁹ On Good Friday the liturgy bursts outdoors: a living Via Crucis threads down Third Street, past barrio murals and the intersection now named Dolores Huerta Square, so the story of the cross is told against spray-painted saints of the labor struggle. Homilies echo with the cadences of liberation theology—Fr. Greg Boyle once urged parishioners to "speak out boldly for the gospel and their own fundamental rights," and today's pastors still quote Gustavo Gutiérrez when they preach about rent justice and migrant dignity.³⁰ Doors stay open long after Mass so that night-shift nurses, unhoused neighbors, or anyone hungry for rice, beans, and belonging can find a seat at the folding tables where faith is served family-style.³¹

Eucharist on the Fifty Blocks The City Forgot. Downtown's neon skyline fades abruptly at Main Street, giving way to the fifty ragged blocks Angelenos call *Skid Row*—a rectangle bounded by Third and Seventh Streets, Alameda and Main, with Fifth Street ("the nickel") as its gritty spine.³² In this half-square-mile live roughly *4,402 unhoused people*—the most concentrated homelessness in the United States, according to the 2022 Greater Los Angeles count.³³ Nights hum with the clang of shopping carts, diesel generators, and LAPD sirens; mornings reveal sidewalks that double as bedrooms and storefront grates repurposed as closets. City "CARE+" clean-ups have carted away tons of needles, refuse, and human waste—one thirteen-day sweep alone removed nearly *five tons*—yet nylon tents bloom back within days.³⁴ Amid the churn, mobile clinicians from USC Street Medicine thread the alleys with stethoscopes, and the Weingart Center hands out hot meals a block from Fifth and San Pedro.³⁵

    29. Dolores Mission School, "School History"; Dolores Mission Church, "Ministries."
        30. Esquivel, "Contemplating Crosses to Bear."
        31. Morrison, "Little Church of Immigrants."
        32. Decker, "Skid Row Streets."
        33. Vives, "$60-Million State Grant."
        34. Zavis, "Los Angeles Skid Row Cleanup."
        35. *USC Street Medicine*, "Addressing a Crisis"; Weingart Center, "Interim

Cracking Babel!

Every six weeks, that same intersection turns into an improvised parish green when a caravan from St. Martin de Porres Catholic Church in Yorba Linda arrives at dawn.[36] The ritual begins the previous Saturday: fifty-plus volunteers fold donated clothes, assemble 300 sack lunches, and pack hygiene kits in the parish hall.[37] At 7 AM Sunday they load the vans and drive thirty-five miles west, parking near the missions and shelters clustered around Fifth and San Pedro. The ministry—nicknamed the "Skid Row Experience"—was born in 2008 with a single case of bottled water; today it fields blankets in winter, coolers of fruit in summer, and roughly *240 care packages* each trip.[38]

Participants include parishioners, youth groups, and members of other outreach organizations. They prepare and distribute food, clothing, and hygiene kits to approximately 240 individuals each visit. Donations come from various sources, including the Knights of Columbus, Lady's Christian League, local food banks, community members, and the church's outreach center. Brendon O'Shea, a recovering alcoholic with over three decades of sobriety, emphasizes that service to others is a key tenet of his recovery program. He notes, "We're making a little bit of a difference."[39] The ministry offers volunteers an opportunity to witness the hardships of life on the streets and to provide support and compassion to those in need—ready to repeat the liturgy of asphalt and mercy six weeks later, until the kingdom is a little harder to overlook in the cracks empire still denies.

Una Casa de Todos. Fifteen miles northeast, in Pasadena, La Fuente Ministries meets in a basement. Planted in 2015 by four millennial seminarians and adopted by the Church of the Nazarene (PazNaz), La Fuente self-conceived as *una casa de todos*—everyone's

---

Housing."

36. Saint Martin de Porres Catholic Church, "Skid Row Ministry."
37. Saint Martin de Porres Catholic Church, "Skid Row Ministry."
38. Saint Martin de Porres Catholic Church, "Skid Row Ministry"; Ponsi, "Banding Together."
39. Ponsi, "Banding Together."

home.⁴⁰ Worship is fully bilingual—English and Spanish braided line for line. Musicians with migration stories from the Middle East, Central America, México, Asia, Euroamerica, and Hawaii layer oud, congas, electric guitars, keyboards, classical violin, and cello into one beat. The preaching comes "in stereo": a preacher and an interpreter volley phrases like jazz solos—liberation theology, diaspora memory, integral mission, gospel lament, decolonial futures. Kids kick a soccer ball up the aisle until the passing of the peace. At the Table the children lead, because the kingdom belongs to such as these. A closing ritual borrows praying candles from abuelas and comadres in protest chants from yesterday's march; evangelicals blink, then breathe it in.

Nobody bolts for the parking lot. A tenured faculty person chats with the landscaper about drought-resistant gardens; the babysitter swaps survival tips with the therapist. Broken English, broken Spanish—whole communion. During the week life happens. La Fuente's members split their time between tenants-rights clinics, ICE-accompaniment shifts, standing vigil against Gaza's bombing, and decolonizing Bible study over tamales at Casitas. La Fuente isn't a Sunday stopover; it's gospel infrastructure—laid in the cracks of empire, crossing the abyssal line, tending the invisible and disposable with stubborn dignity and joy.

No human life is illegal! Rather than erasing difference, these congregations represent a crack in the monocultural layers of power and privilege of metropolitan life. Spirit-scattered diversity, countering assimilationist "melting pot" pressures. They model what I call the Church Without Borders: decentralized, polyphonic, resurgent, and glocally apostolic.⁴¹

---

40. I attend this church. So, this is a witness's account. In addition, see La Fuente Ministries, "Who Are We?"

41. García-Johnson, *Spirit Outside the Gate*, 226–53. For similar sources see also Martinez Jr., *Protestantes*; and Min and Kim, *Religions in Asian America*.

Cracking Babel!

"¡Ya Basta!"

When the Zapatistas rose from the misty highlands of Chiapas at dawn on January 1, 1994, their cry—"¡Ya basta!"—pierced the neoliberal lullaby.[42] But thirty years on, that insurgent shout has matured into a quieter, deeper register. No longer content merely to obstruct the machinery of extraction, Indigenous communities now utter a different verb: re-existir—to re-exist. Re-existence keeps the insurgent "No" alive, yet folds into it a generative "Yes," making space for life to flourish on its own terms. In the agenda of the latest liberation theology, we have moved from *exodus*—fleeing the house of bondage—toward the long, quotidian labor of negotiating *buen vivir* (good living) in *Canaan*—without replicating structural bondage against Canaanites.

Critical theorist Boaventura de Sousa Santos contends, "There is no way of knowing the world better than by anticipating a better world."[43] Anticipation is precisely what Pentecost offers: an eschatological down payment that renders Babel projects absurdly provisional. In the Trump era, the church's vocation is much more than critiquing the circuits of fear, it is to *transfigure* it—turning walls into murals, detention centers into sanctuaries, campaign slogans into prayers of lament and uprising. It is the bold, fluid grace that clears the air, allowing the oppressed, disposable, and persecuted peoples outside Babel's towers to breathe, to rise again, and to re-exist. This is neither the cheap "resurrection hope" of the right nor the liberal illusionistic utopia of the left; it is resurrection realism at the abyssal line, where its triple pillars—colonialism, patriarchy, and capitalism—begin to crack.

The same Spirit who fertilized Mary's womb now "fertilizes the womb of a community and human culture at large."[44] That community is borderless, because the Wild Child of the Trinity respects no jurisdiction nor needs a visa. It is pluriversal, because

---

42. Ejército Zapatista de Liberación Nacional, "First Declaration of the Lacandon Jungle."
43. Santos, *Epistemologies of the South*, 9.
44. García-Johnson, *Spirit Outside the Gate*, 237.

Embracing Fear

the Wild Child of the Trinity delights in many timbres. And it is used to transversing cohesive fear, because decolonial love scatters fear as surely as God once scattered the tower-builders.

So let the towers rise; we shall rise wider in tongues of fire. Let the slogans thunder; we shall answer in a thousand tongues of love. Let the night descend; we shall kindle the Pentecost-pluriversal flame on every threshold closed against the stranger. For to re-existir is to declare with our very breath that Babel is not the last word—Pentecost is.

Discussion Questions

For Community Organizers

- *Spotting Babel in the Neighborhood:* Which current local policies or slogans do you hear echoing the "single tongue of grievance" (e.g., border crackdowns, anti-tenant ordinances, culture warring school boards)? How are people resisting—or internalizing—that script?

- *Fear as Fertile Ground:* The chapter claims fear can be "inverted by grace." Describe a moment when collective anxiety (after a raid, shooting, or policy change) became the seedbed for new solidarity work. What conditions allowed the flip from panic to power?

- *Practicing Re-Existencia:* Borrow one tactic from the Zapatista caracoles, the Sarayaku "Living Forest," or the Guardia Indígena and imagine it transplanted to your zip code. What would have to change—laws, land use, mindsets—for it to thrive?

- *Polyphonic Organizing:* Pentecost frames linguistic multiplicity as a strength. Where does language still create silos in your coalition (ASL, Spanglish, K'iche', youth slang)? Brainstorm a communication practice that turns that babel into a commons.

- *Babel Logic in the Media Stream:* Map one local media narrative that manufactures consent for fortress policies. Which counter-story—podcast, street theater, data visualization—could puncture it, and who must tell that story to shift the public mood?
- *Metrics of Scatter:* If "wins" are not only policy shifts but wider breathing space for pluriversal life, what three indicators (e.g., mutual aid density, police stop reduction, heritage-language signage) would show you're cracking Babel in real time?

For Faith-Based Leaders

- *Decolonizing Pentecost:* On worship day, where do liturgy, preaching, or music still perform the "monoculture of security"? Draft one element (prayer, song, preaching moment) that would signal polyglot, Spirit-led scatter instead.
- *From Fortress to Intercultural Scatter:* The chapter names laundromats, detention-center parking lots, and Skid Row sidewalks as altars. Identify a non-church space your congregation could inhabit sacramentally this year, and predict the pushback you'll face.
- *Prophetic Recordar (Memory) as Eucharist:* Design a communion or Friday prayer liturgy that remembers a local wound (redlined neighborhood, stolen land, internment camp). How might truth-telling at the Table reshape congregational identity?
- *Fear-Training vs. Spirit-Training:* Create a six-week formation rhythm (pilgrimage, street vigils, bilingual Scripture circles) that helps members unlearn indoctrinated fear and practice public joy. What theological language will anchor the shift?
- *Pentecost Budgets:* Audit your next budget cycle against the four "conversions" (polyglot, scatter, glocal partnership,

prophetic memory). Which single line item most embodies Babel anxiety? How could it be redirected toward re-existencia?

- *Liturgical "¡Ya Basta!":* Write a congregational ritual—confession, testimony, children's moment—that lets worshippers utter their own *ya basta* to imperial populism yet moves them from negation to generative practice by week's end.

For the Classroom

- *Babel vs. Pentecost: Textual Mash-Up:* Have students place Genesis 11 and Acts 2 in parallel columns, then annotate how fear, language, and divine action differ. Where does the chapter's thesis—"Pentecost is not reversal but forward achievement"—hold up or break down?

- *Authoritarian Populism Diagnostic:* Using Mudde and Kaltwasser's criteria plus the chapter's "fortress mentality," evaluate a current leader (e.g., Nayib Bukele, Narendra Modi). Is the movement more Babel or Pentecost in shape? Defend with concrete policies.

- *Re-Existencia Case Clinic:* Assign teams one field vignette (Zapatistas, Sarayaku, Guardia Indígena, Coharie, LA urban ministries). Each team identifies (a) the Babel pressure faced, (b) the Pentecost practice adopted, and (c) the measurable cracks produced.

- *Fear-to-Freedom Reflection:* Chomsky writes that intellectual freedom requires decoding "brainwashing under freedom." Ask students to journal one contemporary indoctrination mechanism they personally consume (algorithmic feed, patriotic myth) and outline a liberation practice to counter it.

- *Design-Thinking Sprint: Pentecost City:* In a one-hour sprint, redesign a section of campus or town (housing, transit, public art) using Pentecost principles: pluriversal language, intercultural circulation, shared power. Pitch to a mock city council.

- *Glocal Theology Debate:* Motion: "Dominant-culture churches in the global North can meaningfully lead a 'church without borders.'" Require evidence from Willie Jennings, Boaventura de Sousa Santos, and chapter 5's four conversions.

- *Embodied Senti-Pensar Lab:* Go on a city journey to map sounds, smells, and textures along a local "abyssal line" (gentrification border, policing hotspot). Back in class, interpret findings through the chapter's lens of fear, scatter, and re-existir.

Epilogue

As final preparations were underway to submit this book for publishing, it was June, which is Immigrant Heritage Month in the United States. Ironically, the Trump administration began initiating aggressive, highly irregular ICE raids in Los Angeles (a sanctuary city) during the week before Pentecost Sunday. As a result, tensions were high in my community, and local church as we gathered to worship on June 8, 2025—just hours before President Donald Trump would bypass Governor Gavin Newsom and order two-thousand National Guards to discourage the spread of several protests that were occurring in the Los Angeles areas.

As we gathered for worship that Pentecost Sunday, fear, grief, anger, and confusion hung heavy in the air, but we began, as usual, by calling out to God in honest distress alongside determined praise. Alternating between Spanish and English, the service unfolded as a communal act of resistance and remembrance. Worship moved between solemn invocation and joyful rhythmic *coritos*, calling on the Spirit's presence in times of chaos and need. Through song, the congregation pleaded for the Holy Spirit to comfort and equip it to face uncertain times by rekindling the flame of holy passion within. With voices raised, we created sacred space grounded in intercultural memory, shaped by both suffering and faith.

Communion was framed as a decolonial table—one that rejected exclusion and welcomed all, regardless of age, status, race, or history. Pastoral voices did not shy from the fear and rage in the room. They named grief and confusion in the face of state violence, recognizing its toll on families, schools, and neighborhoods, clearly noting, "That is not of God." Then, the congregation was invited into collective prayerful protest, not as performance, but as spiritual formation. A printed liturgy, *El Credo del Inmigrante* (*The Immigrant's Creed*), was introduced as a guide for the week, offered as both theological witness and communal re-existence.

The Immigrant's Creed[1]

I believe in Almighty God, who guided the people in exile and in exodus,

the God of Joseph in Egypt and Daniel in Babylon, the God of foreigners and immigrants.

I believe in Jesus Christ, a displaced Galilean, who was born away from his people and his home, who fled his country with his parents when his life was in danger.

When he returned to his own country he suffered under the oppression of Pontius Pilate,

the servant of a foreign power.

Jesus was persecuted, beaten, tortured, and unjustly condemned to death.

But on the third day Jesus rose from the dead,

not as a scorned foreigner but to offer us citizenship in God's kingdom.

I believe in the Holy Spirit, the eternal immigrant from God's kingdom among us,

who speaks all languages, lives in all countries, and reunites all races.

I believe that the Church is the secure home for foreigners and for all believers.

I believe that the communion of saints begins when we embrace all God's people

in all their diversity.

---

1. The Immigrant's Creed was written by Rev. Jose Luis Casal, the director of Presbyterian World Mission, an immigrant to the United States from Cuba. The creed is included in *The Book of Common Worship*, 613–14.

Epilogue

> I believe in forgiveness, which makes us all equal before God,
> and in reconciliation, which heals our brokenness.
> I believe that in the Resurrection God will unite us as one people
> in which all are distinct and all are alike at the same time.
> I believe in life eternal, in which no one will be foreigner
> but all will be citizens of the kingdom where God reigns forever and ever. Amen.

When Dr. Amos Yong began his sermon, the people had already preached: Pentecost was not a backdrop but the frame—signaling Spirit not as spectacle, but as sustainer and re-creator. Despite fear, grief, and confusion, we would continue leaning into the Holy Spirit to continue the transforming work of a God who makes *all* things beautifully new—in his time.

Pentecost Today! Building a *Lengua Franca* or Re-Emerging God's Multilingual People?

A Sermon on Genesis 10:29–11:9[2]

Amos Yong

It's always an honor to be invited to share at La Fuente. And when Pastor Marcos asked me a few weeks ago to share on Pentecost

---

2. At the invitation of Rev. Marcos Canales, this sermon was preached at La Fuente Ministries, Pasadena, California, on Pentecost Sunday, June 8, 2025. Thanks to Hermano Canales for welcoming me in this way and for translating my homily, which is the normal approach of this congregation as a bilingual community with each Sunday worship sung and mediated in English and Spanish. Readers who are interested in the full service, of which this message was only a part, can view the recording at the church YouTube channel: https://www.youtube.com/watch?v=qKfPnk1LHRU&t=25s. I have lightly edited the digitally produced transcription and added a few explanatory phrases (using square brackets in the text) and footnotes that also include references to some of my published work (for those who are interested in how my research and

Sunday, as one who has grown up in the Pentecostal church, I said, "Amen!" And when he also shared with me the lectionary text possibilities, I was drawn to the first passage in the Old Testament on the Tower of Babel. And as we've been working on this over the last couple of weeks, periodically I thought to myself, "This is a hard passage to preach on Pentecost Sunday!"

Yet in light of what's been happening over the last few days,[3] perhaps the Lord has prepared this passage for us today. So, as we read the passage and get into it, let us ask the Holy Spirit to speak to us about the relevance of this passage for our lives and work today. Reading from Genesis 10, verse 29, until Genesis 11, verse 9, we are going to be speaking in tongues for the first part of this passage [*several people in the audience laugh at this tongues reference*]:

> 29 Ophir, Havilah, and Jobab; all these were the descendants of Joktan.[4]
>
> 30 The territory in which they lived extended from Mesha in the direction of Sephar, the hill country of the east.
>
> 31 These are the descendants of Shem, by their families, their languages, their lands, and their nations.
>
> 32 These are the families of Noah's sons, according to their genealogies, in their nations, and from these the nations spread abroad on the earth after the flood.
>
> 11:1 Now the whole earth had one language and the same words.

---

scholarship inform my preaching). Upon request, I have also allowed inclusion of minor narrative descriptions to better elucidate context and receptivity of the audience—as this helps to demonstrate attitudes of joyful irony that can be embraced alongside the fear of empire as marginalized communities work toward re-emergence or re-existence.

3. Referring here to the federal deployment of the National Guard and the United States Marines to Los Angeles the weekend of June 6–8, 2025 to chill protests against the (questionable from various perspectives) work of the US Immigrations and Customs Enforcement officers in deportation of undocumented persons, which, as might be expected in a congregation including a large number of Spanish speakers, had been a source of particular consternation.

4. Unless otherwise indicated, Scripture reading and quotations are from the New Revised Standard Version, Updated Edition.

Epilogue

2 And as they migrated from the east, they came upon a plain in the land of Shinar and settled there.

3 And they said to one another, "Come, let us make bricks and fire them thoroughly." And they had brick for stone and bitumen for mortar.

4 Then they said, "Come, let us build ourselves a city and a tower with its top in the heavens, and let us make a name for ourselves; otherwise we shall be scattered abroad upon the face of the whole earth."

5 The Lord came down to see the city and the tower, which mortals had built.

6 And the Lord said, "Look, they are one people, and they have all one language, and this is only the beginning of what they will do; nothing that they propose to do will now be impossible for them.

7 Come, let us go down and confuse their language there, so that they will not understand one another's speech."

8 So the Lord scattered them abroad from there over the face of all the earth, and they left off building the city.

9 Therefore it was called Babel, because there the Lord confused the language of all the earth, and from there the Lord scattered them abroad over the face of all the earth.

May the Lord add his blessing to the word.

I've entitled our few moments together this morning, "Pentecost Today! Building a *Lengua Franca* or Reemerging God's Multilingual People?" I'm using the language of *re-emerge* because that has been the theme [of our Sunday messages] over the last month or two, and I'm glad that you have already been hearing regularly through Pastor Marcos about how the apostles lived in an imperial age. We will get to Acts 2 later, but I hope that we will appreciate Acts 2 in light of what we read here in Genesis.

And it's not just that the entire New Testament was written under imperial Rome, but the entire Old Testament is a story of Israel living amidst different empires. So, I've looked at this notion of *lengua franca*,[5] which actually comes from a few hundred

---

5. *Lengua franca* is the Spanish version of *lingua franca*, which sounds

years ago, arriving into widespread recognition especially during the time of Napoleon [1769–1821] when the French had exerted quite a bit of power over the Mediterranean world. Thus, French became the trade language of the Mediterranean. Across Europe, there were many dozens of languages, but if you wanted to travel and do business, you had to speak French.

Besides English as today's global language, do you know what the second *lengua franca* is around the world today? Spanish is the *lengua franca* across the Americas, especially when you get south of this border. Now, of course, we're going to be speaking Spanish in heaven [*several people in the audience laugh again*]. But for a moment, think about the fact that across Mexico and throughout Latin America, there are hundreds of languages. And south of this border, there's a struggle between the *lengua franca*, which is Spanish, and all of the Indigenous languages. So, on the one hand, when I come to church on Sunday, I want to hear the *lengua hispanica*. But then when I think of all the other Indigenous peoples across the Americas and their struggle against Spanish, I feel both sides of this tension.

That's why, before I start in Genesis 11, I wanted us to read the last few verses of Genesis 10. There is a map I'd like you to look at for a moment.[6] While the details may not be too clear, the green points to Ham, the yellow portion to the lands of the children of Shem, and the orange points to the lands of the descendants of Japheth. So, the last verses that we read from chapter 10 of Genesis talks about the geographic and territorial divisions of the peoples of Shem.

Now, the first twenty-eight verses of Genesis chapter 10 describe how the descendants of Japheth, Ham, and Shem had spread out across these areas. Now, I wanted you to see this division because this tells us about what happened with the children, grandchildren, great-grandchildren, etc., of Noah after the flood.

---

phonetically similar, even among English speakers.

6. A cartographic image which I found at https://afireinmybones.wordpress.com/wp-content/uploads/2011/01/table-of-nations.jpg.

Epilogue

And so, for example, the summary phrases in Genesis chapter 10 say this:

- "These are the descendants of Japheth in their lands, with their own language, by their families, in their nations" (Genesis 10:5);
- "These are the descendants of Ham, by their families, their languages, their lands, and their nations" (Genesis 10:20);
- "These are the descendants of Shem, by their families, their languages, their lands, and their nations" (Genesis 10:31).

Now, if we read all the way from verses 1 to verse 32 of Genesis 10, we would all be speaking in tongues! Genesis 10 actually gives us about seventy different names of peoples, related to lands and languages and cultures, spread out across the [then known] world.

See, in the Jewish understanding, the world consisted of these seventy languages. There is a story that the original translators of the Hebrew Scriptures into Greek numbered seventy persons.[7] But here's the point I want you to take away: that before Genesis 11, the world was already populated by cultural and linguistic diversity. The children of Adam were fulfilling God's invitation given in the garden of Eden, to be fruitful, multiply, and fill the earth. And now the children of Noah, and the grandchildren and the great-grandchildren, and so on, were doing exactly that.

We thus arrive in chapter 11, verse 1: "Now the whole earth had one language and the same words." We might be a bit confused because we just read in chapter 10 that the world had many languages. But the key to understanding this is how the statement is a summary of the coming story. And the key to this summary statement lies in the last phrase. If the author wanted to say only that the whole earth had one language, he[8] would have stopped

---

7. This biblical translation has come to be known as the Septuagint, from the Latin *Septuaginta*, which derives from the Greek *hebdomḗkonta*, both meaning "seventy."

8. Presuming here a male author, which while perhaps an unreflective habit in the sermon, is also probably not historically inaccurate since few

at "had one language," period. But instead, the author says, "had one language and the same words." The "same words" refers [in the Hebrew] not only to a kind of *singleness* but also to a *unitedness*, a common set of words. And the "same words" are also not only *united* but also *elevated* words. Hence, the whole earth had one language and they were united in their words and these words were elevated. What does that sound like? From a linguistic perspective, let me suggest it is a *lengua franca*. From a political perspective these "same words" were a political ideology.

We can see various aspects of this text reflect its referring to a political ideology. Now I want to put up a slide with a timeline on it,[9] and I'm going to go over it quickly. The middle blue timeline gives us 2,000 years of history, which is the 2,000 years before our last 2,000 years, thus before Jesus. We are going to cover all this in five minutes. At the top there's some descriptions about what's happening across this history, and also some biblical developments. The bottom refers to our text and its historical developments. So, where the very top left talks about *prehistory*, that refers to what (from a variety of perspectives) we now call Genesis 1 through 11. These have been called [at least in the West] *prehistorical* "events" because they derive from oral traditions that were handed down and written later.[10] These oral traditions about the nations then perhaps began to be collected during the age of Abraham, Isaac, and Jacob. And when did ancient Israel begin to start writing these down? The story I'm going to tell you is generally agreed upon by most of the people who study these things (even as there are always debates among scholars, which we won't worry about).

---

women would have been scribes during the centuries—on which more in a moment—when this text would have emerged and been developed.

9. For those interested, the referred to and projected timeline can be seen at about the 1:25 mark of the YouTube recording of the sermon: https://www.youtube.com/watch?v=qKfPnk1LHRU.

10. And these oral traditions, of ancient Israel and also other Indigenous cultures, are no less viable self-understandings of peoples around the world even if not recognizable by modern European notions of historicity, which is so much the worse for the latter, as our post- and de-colonial perspectives have begun to clarify.

Epilogue

When we look at it where the timeline says "9 BC or 9 BCE," that would be in the 800s before Christ. What was happening, noted at the top of the timeline, was the beginning of the emergence of what in the history is called the Assyrian Empire. The Assyrian Empire ruled across the known world for over 200 years. When we look at where it says 586, we have another empire emerging: the Babylonian Empire. Israel thus lived not only under the Egyptian Empire, which was in the 2000s, but also under the Assyrians and then under the Babylonians. We can read the whole Old Testament from the perspective of how a small nation was struggling for survival against all of these imperial forces.

Now, if the oral traditions about Genesis 10 and 11 were handed down, the first written versions probably are from the time of the Assyrian Empire. Notice that the story of Babel that we read about locates the events happening in the land of Shinar. This was one of the locations where the Assyrian Empire had its greatest strengths, like a Washington, DC and what that means for us today. Notice also that the text says that this place was then called Babel. While Genesis 10 and 11 were first written down perhaps in about the ninth century, they were then collected into what we now call the Book of the Law, meaning Genesis, Exodus, Leviticus, Numbers, and Deuteronomy, probably over the course of the next 300 or 400 years. Then, we get the final version of this text as we read it after the arrival of the Babylonian Empire. So, when we are reading Genesis 11 and see the reference to the land of Shinar, we can imagine what that meant for people reading that during the time of the Assyrians. And then when we read about Babel at the end, you can imagine what that meant for Israelites reading that in the time of the Babylonians. Hopefully we can see how one story means different things at different times to the people of Israel struggling under different rulers.

I want us now to notice how this text reveals various dimensions of this imperial ideology. How does this text unfold the Israelite perspective on the Assyrians and the Babylonians long before Jesus? The first aspect that we see is the concern about territorial expansion. How many of you know that empires are always looking to expand territory? Think about the language we're hearing about Canada and Greenland today: ". . . as they migrated." [Gen 11:2], that's code for *extending*, for conquering, for gaining territories.

Second, in verses 3–4, we have not only territorial expansion but economic expansion. Whenever it is said, "Come, let us make . . ." or "Come, let us build . . . ," these are also code words for developing economically. Economic might supports political ideology. Think about the economic language that we experience today related to empire. How many of us have heard about and are confused by the word *tariffs*?

But third, in verse 4, besides territorial and economic expansion, there is consolidation of symbolic and spiritual power. So let us not only build economically, not only erect a city which has and manifests economic strength, but construct a tower which has additional symbolic purposes. The tower was intended to reach to the heavens. While this is metaphorical, what do *the heavens* represent? The heavenlies represent cosmic power: rooted in the local region, but enabling surveillance that extends way beyond toward the horizons, effectively exerting authority over the known world. This would be a consolidation of communicative power, of legal power, and of political power.

Finally, then, there is (fourth) sociocultural capital or power. The text exactly says that, "otherwise we shall be scattered abroad upon the face of the whole earth" [Gen 11:4b]. The concern was to make a name for themselves. But let me give a little bit of clarification. The text indicates that they felt a need to make a name for themselves *otherwise they would experience being scattered, rather than feel united,* across the face of the earth. See, the concern is not about being situated across the face of the earth. The Babelians sought territorial increase. They wanted to be across the face of the earth. They just did not want to be disunited across these territories. Instead, they want to be united and elevated across the known world.

Understand this: dispersal in a disempowered and fragmented sense means that local languages reign across the face of the earth. To be dispersed across the world in a united sense, however, is to be able to exercise control wherever that unity is exertable. The latter is to be able to impose a *lengua franca*, or in this case, a *lengua Assyriana*, or in the fifth century BCE, a *lengua Babylonia*. Yes, one language, but more important, one lip,[11] or "the same words": one united and elevated way of thinking and living, one prioritized ideology, one normative way of being in the world. So, if successful, ideology grows as territories are expanded, wealth is accumulated, authority is centralized, and the *lengua franca*, the ideology, is embraced.

So, today, when we receive "truths" from Truth Social,[12] that is an attempt to exert social, cultural, and political power. A political ideology can be spoken in many languages, but they communicate that one "normative truth," no matter what the real truths are in the world. A powerful political ideology dictates its own "truth," that when internalized by the people become "the same words."

So how does ancient Israel existing under Assyrian and Babylonian threats then envision God's intervention? Notice what God says in verse 6: "nothing that they propose to do will now be impossible for them." God is seeing the exertion and centralization of power, symbolized by what is happening in terms of building and economics, and in terms of sociocultural capital that is being mobilized by the Assyrians. And God says in verse 7, "let us go down and confuse their language there, so they will not understand one another's speech." Notice it's not that they won't understand the language—you can always have translations—but rather the goal is to undermine the ideology, to subvert the unitary truth that the political empire is attempting to proclaim. How do we resist empire? God's word confuses human and imperial ideology.

More directly, God is re-empowering the languages and witnesses of all of the peoples spread out across the earth that Genesis 10 already described. With the confusion of the Babelian political ideology, God is reminding the empire that there were many

11. Which is the more wooden and literal translation of the Hebrew; thus also the King James Version translates "one speech" and the New International Version "a common speech."

12. See https://truthsocial.com/.

pre-existing languages. There were and are many cultures and many people groups, speaking many languages and bearing witness to many perspectives. To reinforce this message, God then chooses very small and minoritized communities in the face of imperial aspirations and programs. At the end of chapter 11 of Genesis, guess who we are introduced to?

God picks one out of the seventy tribes or peoples: that of Abraham's. His descendants recognized that they were nobodies, that they were just a small group in Palestine surrounded by many other people. They understood they had done nothing important and were undeserving of any kind of recognition, as can be read elsewhere in the Old Testament.[13] The ancient Israelites asked, effectively, why did you choose us God? God "elects" these Aramaic peoples and elevates their (minoritized) language. This anticipates the Day of Pentecost narrative that tells us every language still counts, that every people group and every cultural group and geographic region still counts, having the freedom of life and expression.

Acts 2 says this:

Now there were devout Jews from every people under heaven living in Jerusalem. And at this sound the crowd gathered and was bewildered, because each one heard them speaking in the native language of each. Amazed and astonished, they asked, "Are not all these who are speaking Galileans? And how is it that we hear, each of us, in our own native language? Parthians, Medes, Elamites, and residents of Mesopotamia, Judea and Cappadocia, Pontus and Asia, Phrygia and Pamphylia, Egypt and the parts of Libya belonging to Cyrene, and visitors from Rome, both Jews and proselytes, Cretans and Arabs—in our own languages we hear them speaking about God's deeds of power" (Acts 2:5–11).[14]

God empowers us in our languages first and foremost to worship him: that is the answer to Assyria and Babylon. Yes, God has

---

13. E.g., Deuteronomy 7:7–8.

14. I have provided sociocultural, racial-ethnic, and political readings of this portion of the Acts 2 narrative in many places, a good number of them gathered in my *Heteroglossic Spirit*, parts II and III.

chosen the Jews first, but now with Pentecost, God has also chosen the Greeks, or the gentiles, all who were not Jews, including me and you, and wherever your values, experiences, and perspectives come from.

I am an immigrant, too. I was born in the country of Malaysia, to Chinese immigrants in Malaysia.[15] So, now I'm a Chinese-Malaysian-American something [*the audience chuckles*] and since I'm married to a Tejana-Mexicana-Americana [*more laughter*], our kids are . . . [*additional laughter*] . . . Pentecost! [*The audience erupts with clapping, cheers, and more laughter.*] Amen? To the Jews first, and also to all the gentiles, which means to all the indigenous peoples of the world. The seventy nations of the book of Genesis are now the 7,000 languages belonging to different people spread across around the world that we know about today, half of which are in peril.[16]

Genesis 10 told us that this diversity of peoples, cultures, and languages is exactly the way God intended it: to be spread out across the world, in different contexts, developing distinct cultures, forming unique ways of life in their own languages. We know that the languages of the world reflect the different parts of the world that people live in: different territories, different climates. If you live along an oceanfront, then you have a lot more language for the different kinds of aquatic life forms. If you live in the Andean mountains of Peru, then you have languages that reflect the life and the vegetation and the animals that live in that part of the world.[17] God's answer to the Assyrian and Babylonian empires of this world is a multicultural, multi-ethnic, and multi-linguistic community that is called the church!

---

15. I tell more about my journey in "From Every Tribe, Language, People, and Nation."

16. For more on my perspective on Genesis 10—11 in relationship to language endangerment, see the second section of my essay, "Many Tongues, Many Biocultural Niches."

17. See my lecture, "The Bible's Story of Creation and Renewal." Thanks to my wife, Alma Yong, and to Oscar García-Johnson for help with the translation of the PowerPoint slides.

The church receives its mandate in part as children of Abraham the nobody. The church receives the Abrahamic mandate by the power of Jesus and his Spirit, to live out its unique calling across the different cultures and via various languages around the world, always evolving as hybridity, which our own lives reflect. As a multilingual community, empowering local languages and dialects, La Fuente is a wonderful example with our bilingualness. Remember now we are two *lengua francas* (Spanish and English), so how do we nurture and encourage other more minoritized languages in our midst as well?

We are not only a bilingual and intercultural community, but we're also an intergenerational community. I loved it last week when Elias[18] came up and translated for the congregation. We know that when Peter was called upon to explain Pentecost to the crowd, he draws upon the prophet Joel: "In the last days it will be, God declares, that I will pour out my Spirit upon all flesh, and your sons and your daughters shall prophesy, and your young men shall see visions, and your old men shall dream dreams" (Acts 2:17; cf. Joel 2:28). Elias and his papa were both declaring the wondrous works of God in their own way.

So, each week here at La Fuente, we respond to empire first and foremost by declaring the wondrous works of God in our worship. Our worship comes out of our culture, our experience, our language, and our perspective. And we declare what from our perspective, experience, culture, and languages is God's intention for the church today. This is God's normative invitation for us, under any empire and even at this imperial moment.

And I know about the normativity of Pentecost because it will continue eternally. I want to close by inviting us to look at a couple of verses in the book of Revelation. In Revelation chapter 5 verse 9, the twenty-four elders "took up a new song, saying, 'You are worthy to take the scroll and open its seals, because you were slain, and by your blood you purchased for God persons from every tribe, language, people, and nation . . .'" Revelation chapter 7 says something similar. John sees in his vision of the 144,000, "a great

---

18. Elias is the nine-year-old son of Pastor Marcos and Andrea.

Epilogue

crowd that no one could number. They were from every nation, tribe, people, and language. They were standing before the throne and before the Lamb" (Rev 7:9).[19] I don't know, maybe Spanish will be a little louder in heaven [*several people in the audience laugh*]. Maybe there will be some competition between the Spanish and English and who knows, Mandarin.

But what about all of the Indigenous languages across Latin America? What about all of the dialects of and languages across Central Asia? How will all of that resound before the throne of God? If I had been more informed as I was growing up and raising our kids I would have probably worked harder with my wife to teach them more than one language. I was raised in Malaysia as part of the extension of the British Empire so my parents said, "Well, if we are going to work with the American missionaries, we should raise our children to speak English well." Unfortunately, the result was that I never learned the language of my grandparents when I was growing up. I learned the *lengua franca*. I wish I was more bilingual. Don't underestimate what you're able to do by nurturing your children in multiple languages. I think my wife has an amazing calling to teach high school Spanish to students. Not only is it going to be really prevalent in heaven as we've already talked about, but, again, to empower our children with another language gives them voice and capacity to bear witness in multiple perspectives. It is to empower potentially different ways of being in the world that could be resistant to any political ideology. Yes, the *lengua franca* can be a helpful mode of communication. But it could also be used imperially to marginalize minoritized groups.

Pray with me as we close.

Lord Jesus, continue to pour out your Holy Spirit in our community. Continue to pour out your Spirit in our extended communities. Continue to pour out your Spirit upon the community in the LA area. And continue to pour your Spirit across the transnational communities represented by your people in this room and online. Give us your Spirit in our daily lives. Come Holy

---

19. For discussion of these texts, including in relationship to their variant in Rev 10:11, see my *Revelation*, 89–90, 110–13, and 137–38.

Spirit, empower us to bear witness to God's deeds of power. Enable us to testify out of our experiences and to tell of your good works in light of what you've done in our family, in our cultures, in our church. In Jesus' name, amen.

And then we, the people, continued our worshipful work of resistance and re-existence by sharing a meal and embracing fear and hope together.

Bibliography

Allen, R. E. *Plato's 'Republic': A Critical Guide.* Cambridge: Cambridge University Press, 2012.
Amnesty International. "They Did Not Treat Us Like People: Race and Migration-Related Torture and Ill-Treatment of Haitians Seeking Safety in the U.S." September 22, 2022. https://www.amnesty.org/en/documents/amr51/5895/2022/en/.
Annas, Julia. *An Introduction to Plato's Republic.* Oxford: Oxford University Press, 1981.
Arendt, Hannah. *The Origins of Totalitarianism.* New York: Harcourt, 1973.
Art, David. "The Myth of Global Populism." *Perspectives on Politics* 20, no. 4, 2020, 999–1011.
Asch, Solomon E. "Opinions and Social Pressure." *Scientific American* 193, no. 5 (1955) 31–35.
Atkins, Jed W. *Cicero on Politics and the Limits of Reason.* Cambridge: Cambridge University Press, 2013.
Barber, Benjamin. *Strong Democracy: Participatory Politics for a New Age.* Berkeley: University of California Press, 2004.
Bates, Crispin. *Subalterns and Raj: South Asia since 1600.* Abingdon: Routledge, 2007.
Benne, Robert, and Phillip Hefner, *Defining America: A Christian Critique of the American Dream.* Minneapolis: Fortress, 1974.
Berde, Stuart. *Politics and Prayers: The Role of Evangelicalism in Coharie Tribal History.* Pembroke, NC: Lumbee River Legal Services, 1982.
Berlin, Isaiah. *Four Essays on Liberty.* Oxford: Oxford University Press, 1969.
Bobo, Lawrence, and Franklin D. Gilliam, Jr. "Race, Sociopolitical Participation, and Black Empowerment." *American Political Science Review* 84 (1982) 377–89.
The Book of Common Worship. Louisville: Westminster John Knox, 2018.
Brueggemann, Walter. *Genesis.* Louisville: John Knox, 1982.
Burkert, Walter. *Greek Religion.* Translated by John Raffan. Cambridge: Harvard University Press, 1985.

Bibliography

Butler, Geo E. *The Croatan Indians of Sampson County, North Carolina: Their Origin and Racial Status: A Plea for Separate Schools.* Durham, NC: The Seeman Printery, 1916.

Carothers, Christopher. "The Surprising Instability of Competitive Authoritarianism." *Journal of Democracy* 29 (2018) 129–35.

Castaldo, Antonino. "Populism and Competitive Authoritarianism in Turkey." *Southeast European and Black Sea Studies* 18 (2018) 467–87.

Chomsky, Noam. "The Manufacture of Consent." In *The Chomsky Reader*, edited by James Peck, 121–36. New York: Pantheon, 1987.

———. *Media Control: The Spectacular Achievements of Propaganda.* New York: Seven Stories, 2002.

———. *Necessary Illusions: Thought Control in Democratic Societies.* Boston: South End, 1989.

Chomsky, Noam, and Edward S. Herman. *Manufacturing Consent: The Political Economy of the Mass Media.* New York: Pantheon, 1998.

Christerson, Brad, Alexia Salvatierra, Robert Chao Romero, and Nancy Wang Yuen. *God's Resistance: Mobilizing Faith to Defend Immigrants.* New York: NYU Press, 2023.

Chuang, D. J. "Chapter 9: Churches that Last for Generations." MultiAsian. Church, September 6, 2016. https://multiasian.church/chapter-9-churches-that-last-for-generations/.

———. *MultiAsian.Church: A Future for Asian Americans in a Multiethnic World.* N.p.: CreateSpace, 2016.

Cicero. *De Officiis.* Translated by Walter Miller. Cambridge: Harvard University Press, 1913.

Clemente, Édgar H. "Mexico's Zapatista Rebel Movement Says It Is Dissolving Its 'Autonomous Municipalities.'" Associated Press, November 6, 2023. https://apnews.com/article/mexico-indigenous-zapatista-rebels-violence-04006895dc4bd430b4b957d459551a12.

Cohen, Rachel M. "Trump's First 100 Days Show Project 2025's Blueprint in Action." *Vox*, May 12, 2025. https://www.vox.com/politics/2025/5/12/project-2025-trump-executive-orders.

Coharie Tribe. "History: Coharie Indian Tribe—About the People." https://coharietribe.org/history/#:~:text=The%20Coharie%20Indian%20Tribe%20has,of%20North%20Carolina%20since%201971.

Consejo Regional Indígena del Cauca (CRIC). "La Guardia Indígena: Defensa de la Vida, la Cultura y la Paz." *CRIC Cauca Reports*, March 2024. https://www.cric-colombia.org.

Corrales, Javier. "Why Populism Is the Sugar, Salt, and Fat of Our Politics . . . with Variations." *American Behavioral Scientist* 68 (2024) 1804–14.

Corte Interamericana de Derechos Humanos. *Caso Pueblo Indígena Kichwa de Sarayaku vs. Ecuador* (Sentencia de 27 de junio de 2012). San José, Costa Rica: CorteIDH, 2012.

Cortina, Adela. *Aporophobia: Why We Reject the Poor Instead of Helping Them.* Princeton: Princeton University Press, 2022.

Bibliography

Das, Saswat Samay, and Deepak Mathew. "India after Modi: Populism and the Right." *Rethinking Marxism* 34 (2022) 433–35.

Decker, Twilight. "Skid Row Streets Are Home No Longer." *Los Angeles Times*, October 29, 2000. https://www.latimes.com/archives/la-xpm-2000-oct-29-me-43954-story.html?_gl=1*1keenoi*_gcl_au*MTYzMTc3MzkwMS4x NzQ4NTc5ODI1.

De La Torre, Carlos. "Populism in Latin America." In *The Oxford Handbook of Populism*, edited by Cristóbal Rovira Kaltwasser et al., 195–211. Oxford: Oxford University Press, 2017.

De La Torre, Miguel A. *Embracing Hopelessness*. Minneapolis: Fortress, 2017.

———. *Resisting Apartheid America: Living the Badass Gospel*. Grand Rapids: Eerdmans, 2023.

Dolores Mission Church. "About." https://dolores-mission.org/about/.

———. "Ministries: Base Communities (CEBs). " https://dolores-mission.org/ministries.

Dolores Mission School. "School History: Intergenerational Change for Over 74 Years." https://doloresmissionschool.org/school-history.

Downs, Anthony. *An Economic Theory of Democracy*. New York: Harper, 1957.

Dunne, Sierra. "The Coharie Tribe: Soil, Sorghum, and Sovereignty." Video. YouTube. 15 min. 9 sec. May 7, 2019. https://youtu.be/KouD8kGbInM?si=G6tAui1U_BWlt9YC.

Durkheim, Émile. *The Division of Labor in Society*. New York: The Free Press, 1997.

Dussel, Enrique. *Ethics of Liberation in the Age of Globalization and Exclusion*. Translated by Eduardo Mendieta, et al. Durham, NC: Duke University Press, 2013.

Djupe, Paul, and Ryan Burge. "Regular churchgoing doesn't make Trump voters more moderate. It makes them more enthusiastic for Trump." *The Washington Post*, October 9, 2018. https://www.washingtonpost.com/news/monkey-cage/wp/2018/10/09/regular-churchgoing-doesnt-make-trump-voters-more-moderate-it-makes-them-more-enthusiastic-for-trump/.

Ejército Zapatista de Liberación Nacional. "First Declaration of the Lacandon Jungle." January 1, 1994. https://static1.squarespace.com/static/5e2b1eb9509d4862f6e435er/t/6317ccf314c5821e5515ddd9/1662504182967/1994%2BFirst%2BSecond%2Band%2BThird%2BDeclaration%2B-%2BZapatistas.pdf.

Esquivel, Paloma. "Contemplating Crosses to Bear." *Los Angeles Times*, March 22, 2008. https://www.latimes.com/archives/la-xpm-2008-mar-22-me-beliefs22-story.html#:~:text=All%20around%20them%2C%20men%20and,to%20the%20theological%2C%20organizers%20said.&text=Just%20before%20worshipers%20started%20on,cause%20families%20to%20be%20separated.%E2%80%9D.

Evergreen Baptist Church of Los Angeles. "About." https://ebcla.org/about.

Bibliography

Everitt, Anthony. *Cicero: The Life and Times of Rome's Greatest Politician*. New York: Random House, 2003.

Fanon, Frantz. *Black Skin, White Masks*. New York: Grove, 1967.

―――. *The Wretched of the Earth*. New York: Grove, 1963.

Farrer, Austin. *Faith and Speculation: An Essay in Philosophical Theology*. London: A. & C. Black, 1967.

Festinger, Leon. *A Theory of Cognitive Dissonance*. Stanford, CA: Stanford University Press, 1957.

Frank, Erich. *Philosophical Understanding and Religious Truth*. London: Oxford University Press, 1945.

French, David. "Why Fundamentalists Love Trump." *New York Times*, December 7, 2023. https://www.nytimes.com/2023/12/07/opinion/donald-trump-fundamentalists-evangelical.html.

Gal, Daniel. "The Challenges of an Ethnic Democracy: Populism, Netanyahu, and Israel's Path." *MaRBLe* 3 (2018) 1–18.

García-Johnson, Oscar. *Introducción a la Teología del Nuevo Mundo: El Quehacer Teológico en el Siglo XXI*. Barcelona, España: Editorial CLIE, 2022.

―――. *The Mestizo/a Community of the Spirit: A Postmodern Latino/a Ecclesiology*. Eugene, OR: Pickwick, 2009.

―――. "The Politics of the *Espíritu*: Ethics as Recognition-Assemblage-Decolonial Healing." In *T&T Clark Handbook of Political Theology*, edited by Rubén Rosario Rodríguez, 355–72. New York: T&T Clark, 2019.

―――. *Spirit Outside the Gate: Decolonial Pneumatologies of the American Global South*. Downers Grove, IL: IVP Academic, 2019.

Gill, M. N. "Plato on True and False Religion." *Phronesis* 28 (1983) 98–105.

Grady, Don Avasco. "The Coharie Indians of Sampson County, North Carolina: A Collection of Their Oral Folk History." Thesis, University of North Carolina at Chapel Hill, 1981.

Graham, David A. "The Trump Supporters Who Didn't Take Him at His Word." *The Atlantic* (blog), February 12, 2025. https://www.theatlantic.com/newsletters/archive/2025/02/the-trump-supporters-who-didnt-take-him-at-his-word/681674/.

Gushee, David, and Glen Stassen. *Kingdom Ethics: Following Jesus in Contemporary Context*. 2nd ed. Grand Rapids: Eerdmans, 2016.

Halmai, Gábor. "Populism, Authoritarianism, and Constitutionalism." *German Law Journal* 20 (2019) 296–313.

Harvey, David. *A Brief History of Neoliberalism*. Oxford: Oxford University Press, 2005.

Harrington, James. *The Commonwealth of Oceana and A System of Politics*. Cambridge: Cambridge University Press, 1992.

Heritage Foundation. *Mandate for Leadership: The Conservative Promise*. Washington, DC: The Heritage Foundation, 2023. https://www.project2025.org.

Homer. *The Iliad*. Translated by Richmond Lattimore. Chicago: University of Chicago Press, 1951.

Bibliography

———. *The Odyssey*. Translated by Robert Fagles. New York: Penguin, 1996

Human Rights Watch. "U.S. Deliberately Inflicting Harm on Returned Haitians." October 5, 2021. https://www.hrw.org/news/2021/10/05/us-deliberately-inflicting-harm-returned-haitians.

Hurtado, Lina Maria, and Carlos Walter Porto-Gonçalves. "Resistir y Re-existir." *GEOgraphia* 24 no. 53 (2022) 19–33.

Ignatiev, Noel. *How the Irish Became White*. New York: Routledge, 1995.

Jennings, Willie James. *The Christian Imagination: Theology and the Origins of Race*. New Haven: Yale University Press, 2010.

Johnson, Edward. *Wonder-Working Providence, 1628–1651*. Edited by J. Franklin Jameson. New York: Charles Scribner's Sons, 1910.

Kang, K. Connie. "Building on the Gospel of Inclusion." *Los Angeles Times*, December 8, 2001. https://www.latimes.com/archives/la-xpm-2001-dec-08-me-12829-story.html.

Kaplan, Amy. *Our American Israel: The Story of an Entangled Alliance*. Cambridge: Harvard University Press, 2018.

Kim, Jung Ha Kim, and Pyong Gap Min. *Religions in Asian America: Building Faith Communities*. Bloomington: Indiana University Press, 2002.

Korecki, Natasha. "Project 2025's Architect Is Now Directing Trump's Policy Machine." *Politico*, March 15, 2025. https://www.politico.com/news/2025/03/15/russ-vought-trump-policy-2025-116578.

Kruse, Kevin M. *One Nation Under God: How Corporate America Invented Christian America*. New York: Basic, 2015.

La Fuente Ministries. "Who are we?" https://www.paznaz.org/lafuenteministries/.

Lee, Hak Joon. *God and Community Organizing: A Covenantal Approach*. Waco, TX: Baylor University Press, 2020.

Levitsky, Steven, and Lucan Way. "The New Competitive Authoritarianism." *Journal of Democracy* 31 (2020) 51–65.

Liggett, Billy. "Survivance." *Campbell Magazine*, December 7, 2022. https://magazine.campbell.edu/articles/survivance/.

Lignum Crucis Productions. *Our People: The Coharie*. August 20, 2015. Video interview, funded by the Museum of the Southeast American Indian and University of Chapel Hill at Pembroke. 28 min. 29 sec. https://www.youtube.com/watch?v=ffC7ZxRqPCs.

Los Angeles Homeless Services Authority. "2023 Greater Los Angeles Homeless Count—Downtown/Skid Row Data Summary." https://www.lahsa.org/news?article=927-lahsa-releases-results-of-2023-greater-los-angeles-homeless-count#:~:text=LOS%20ANGELES%20E2%80%93%20The%202023%20Greater,to%20an%20estimated%2046%2C260%20people.

Machiavelli, Niccolò. *The Prince*. 2nd ed. Translated by Harvey C. Mansfield. Chicago: University of Chicago Press, 1998.

MacIntyre, Alasdair. *After Virtue: A Study in Moral Theory*. 3rd ed. Notre Dame: University of Notre Dame Press, 2007.

Maclure, Jocelyn. *Quebec Identity: The Challenge of Pluralism*. Montreal: McGill-Queen's University Press, 2003.

Bibliography

Mamdani, Mahmood. *Citizen and Subject: Contemporary Africa and the Legacy of Late Colonialism.* Princeton: Princeton University Press, 1996.

Martell-Otero, Loida, et al. *Latina Evangélicas: A Theological Survey from the Margins.* Eugene, OR: Cascade, 2013.

Martin, Michel. "Hispanic Evangelical Leader Looks Ahead to the Incoming Trump Administration." *Morning Edition*, NPR, December 16, 2024. https://www.npr.org/2024/12/16/nx-s1-5206594/hispanic-evangelical-leader-looks-ahead-to-the-incoming-trump-administration.

Martinez, Juan Francisco, Jr. *Los Protestantes: An Introduction to Latino Protestantism in the United States.* Westport: Praeger, 2011.

McCormick, John. *Machiavellian Democracy.* Cambridge: Cambridge University Press, 2011.

McCrummen, Stephanie. "The Army of God Comes Out of the Shadows." *The Atlantic*, January 9, 2025. https://www.theatlantic.com/magazine/archive/2025/02/new-apostolic-reformation-christian-movement-trump/681092-/.

Mignolo, Walter. "Decolonizing Western Epistemology/Building Decolonial Epistemology." In *Decolonizing Epistemologies: Latino/a Theology and Philosophy*, edited by Ada María Isasi-Díaz and Eduardo Mendieta, 19–43. New York: Fordham University Press, 2012.

Mill, John Stuart. *On Liberty.* London: Longman, Roberts, & Green Co., 1859.

Min, Pyong Gap, and Jung Ha Kim. *Religions in Asian America: Building Faith Communities.* Walnut Creek, CA: AltaMira, 2002.

Miranda, Roberto S. *En La Tierra de Los Peregrinos: La Iglesia Evangélica Hispana Y Su Llamado Redentor.* Río Piedras, PR: Palabra y más, 2009.

Mitchell, Thomas N. *Cicero: The Senior Statesman.* New Haven: Yale University Press, 1991.

Morrison, Pat. "Little Church of Immigrants Stands Up to Be Counted." *Los Angeles Times*, June 30 1987. https://www.latimes.com/archives/la-xpm-1987-6-30-me-1224-story.html.

Mudde, Cas. *The Far Right Today.* Cambridge: Polity, 2019.

Mudde, Cas, and Cristóbal Rovira Kaltwasser. *Populism: A Very Short Introduction.* Oxford: Oxford University Press, 2017.

Ndofirepi, Amasa P., and Ephraim T. Gwaravanda. "Boaventura de Sousa Santos' Epistemologies of the South: The Case of Universities in Africa." In *African Higher Education in the 21st Century: Epistemological, Ontological and Ethical Perspectives*, 90–105. Leiden: Brill, 2021.

Nortey, Justin. "Most White Americans Who Regularly Attend Worship Services Voted for Trump in 2020." Pew Research Center, August 30 2021. https://www.pewresearch.org/short-reads/2021/08/30/most-white-americans-who-regularly-attend-worship-services-voted-for-trump-in-2020/.

O'Harrow, Robert, Jr., et al. "Trump Reinstates Schedule F, Aiming to Reshape the Federal Workforce." *Washington Post*, April 8, 2025. https://www.washingtonpost.com/politics/2025/04/08/schedule-f-trump-federal-workers.

Bibliography

Panotto, Nicolás. "Christian Zionism as Geopolitics and Public Theology: A Latin American Perspective." *Contending Modernities*, September 26, 2024. https://contendingmodernities.nd.edu/global-currents/christian-zionism-latin-america/.

Paxton, Robert. *The Anatomy of Fascism*. New York: Alfred A. Knopf, 2004.

Plato. *The Republic*. 2nd ed. Translated by Allan Bloom. New York: Basic, 1991.

Ponsi, Lou. "Banding Together to Give Back: Spotlight on the Skid Row Ministry at Saint Martin de Porres." *Orange County Catholic*, November 23, 2022. https://www.occatholic.com/banding-together-to-give-back/.

Prashad, Vijay. "Dr. Victor Frankenstein Disavows His Monster: The Second Newsletter (2025)." Tricontinental Institute for Social Research, January 9, 2025. https://thetricontinental.org/newsletterissue/struggles-illuminate-the-path-forward/.

———. "Resist, My People, Resist: The Fifty-Second Newsletter (2024)." *Tricontinental: Institute for Social Research*. December 26, 2024. https://thetricontinental.org/newsletterissue/palestine-and-struggle-in-the-new-year/.

Price, Simon R. F. *Rituals and Power: The Roman Imperial Cult in Asia Minor*. Cambridge: Cambridge University Press, 1984.

Pueblo Originario Kichwa de Sarayaku. *Kawsak Sacha: Selva Viviente*. Declaration presented 2018, reaffirmed 2021. https://sarayaku.org.

Raheb, Mitri. *Decolonizing Palestine: The Land, the People, the Bible*. Maryknoll, NY: Orbis, 2023.

Restall, Matthew. *Seven Myths of the Spanish Conquest*. Oxford: Oxford University Press, 2003.

Rodriguez, Samuel. "Hispanic Voters Shift Right; Pastor Samuel Rodriguez Explains Why." Interview by Michael Huckabee. *Huckabee Today*, December 17, 2024. https://youtu.be/FnhDXFnj6wA?si=Y6cuBLEf6shP2gbL.

———. "Trump's Mass Deportation Plan? Pastor Samuel Rodriguez Explains." The Christian Broadcasting Network, video interview. https://cbn.com/video/trumps-mass-deportation-plan-pastor-sam-rodriguez-explains.

Rousseau, Jean-Jacques. *Discourse on Inequality: On the Origin and Basis of Inequality among Men*. Auckland, NZ: Floating, 2009.

———. *The Social Contract*. Translated by Maurice Cranston. London: Penguin, 1968.

Saint Martin de Porres Catholic Church. "Skid Row Ministry." https://smdpyl.org/skidrow.

Santos Cid, Alejandro. "Mexico's Zapatistas Warn Chiapas Is on 'the Verge of Civil War.'" *El País* (US English), June 1, 2023. https://english.elpais.com/international/2023-6-01/mexicos-zapatistas-warn-chiapas-is-on-the-verge-of-civil-war.html.

Santos, Boaventura de Sousa. "The Alternative to Utopia is Myopia." *Politics & Society* 48 (2020) 567–84.

Bibliography

———. "Beyond Abyssal Thinking: From Global Lines to Ecologies of Knowledges." *Review* 30 (2007) 45–89.

———. *Democratizing Democracy: Beyond the Liberal Democratic Canon.* London: Verso, 2007.

———. "Democracy in Dispute." An interview with Boaventura de Sousa Santos by Roque Urbieta Hernandez and Fabiola Navarro. openDemocracy, October 26, 2016. https://www.opendemocracy.net/en/democraciaabierta/democracy-in-di/.

———. *The End of the Cognitive Empire: The Coming of Age of Epistemologies of the South.* Durham, NC: Duke University Press, 2018.

———. *Epistemologies of the South: Justice against Epistemicide.* Kindle ed. Taylor & Francis, 2014.

———. "Epistemologies of the South and the Future." *From the European South: A Transdisciplinary Journal* (2016) 17–29.

———. "Fascism 2.0: An Intensive Course." *Critical Legal Thinking*, November 19, 2020. https://criticallegalthinking.com/2020/11/19/fascism-2-0-an-intensive-course/.

———. *If God Were a Human Rights Activist.* Stanford, CA: Stanford University Press, 2015.

———. "A New Vision of Europe: Learning from the Global South." In *Demodiversity: Toward Post-Abyssal Democracies*, edited by Boaventura de Sousa Santos and José Manuel Mendes, 31–53. New York: Routledge, 2020.

———. "The Politics of Translation: Boaventura de Sousa Santos—Learned Ignorance." Center for Advanced Studies "CAS SEE," University of Rijeka, January 17, 2023. YouTube video, 28 min. 8 sec. https://www.youtube.com/watch?v=LdWzD-hMhW8.

———. "Postcolonialism, Decoloniality, and Epistemologies of the South." In *Oxford Research Encyclopedia of Literature.* Oxford: Oxford University Press, 2021.

———. *Reinventing Democracy.* Coimbra: Centro de Estudos Sociais, 1999.

———. "The Resilience of Abyssal Exclusions in Our Societies: Toward a Post-Abyssal Law." *Tilburg Law Review* 22 (2017) 237–58.

———. "Toward an Aesthetics of the Epistemologies of the South: Manifesto in Twenty-Two Theses." In *Knowledges Born in the Struggle: Constructing the Epistemologies of the Global South*, edited by Boaventura de Sousa Santos and Maria Paula Meneses, 115–25. London: Routledge, 2019.

Santos, Boaventura de Sousa, and José Manuel Mendes. "Introduction." In *Demodiversity: Toward Post-Abyssal Democracies*, edited by Boaventura de Sousa Santos and José Manuel Mendes, 1–28. New York: Routledge, 2020.

Sassen, Saskia. *Territory, Authority, Rights: From Medieval to Global Assemblages.* Princeton: Princeton University Press, 2006.

Servicio Internacional para la Paz (SIPAZ). "The Path of the Caracol Towards Autonomy." *SIPAZ Report 10*, March 2005. https://www.sipaz.org/in-focus-the-path-of-the-caracol-towards-autonomy/?lang=en.

Bibliography

Shear, Michael D., and Charlie Savage. "Trump Administration Pushes Education Cuts in Line with Heritage Blueprint." *New York Times*, April 20, 2025. https://www.nytimes.com/2025/04/20/us/politics/education-department-project-2025.html.

Skocpol, Theda. *States and Social Revolutions: A Comparative Analysis of France, Russia, and China*. Cambridge: Cambridge University Press, 1979.

Spector, Stephen. *Evangelicals and Israel: The Story of American Christian Zionism*. Oxford: Oxford University Press, 2009.

Strauss, Leo. *Natural Right and History*. Chicago: University of Chicago Press, 1953.

Tajfel, Henri, and John C. Turner. "An Integrative Theory of Intergroup Conflict." In *The Social Psychology of Intergroup Relations*, edited by William G. Austin and Stephen Worchel, 33–47. Monterey, CA: Brooks/Cole, 1979.

Tamayo Acosta, Juan José. "Decolonizing Knowledge: Boaventura de Sousa Santos' Vision." Meer, November 20, 2024. https://www.meer.com/81190-decolonizing-boaventura-de-sousa-santos-vision.

Tarrow, Sidney. *Power in Movement: Social Movements and Contentious Politics*. 3rd ed. Cambridge: Cambridge University Press, 2011.

Tinker, George E. *Spirit and Resistance: Political Theology and American Indian Liberation*. Minneapolis: Fortress, 2004.

USC Street Medicine. "Addressing a Crisis." Keck School of Medicine of University of Southern California. https://keck.usc.edu/street-medicine/.

Vives, Ruben. "$60-million state grant to aid L.A. County in expanding homeless services in Skid Row." *Los Angeles Times*, June 26, 2023. https://www.latimes.com/california/story/2023-6-26/60-million-state-grant-to-aid-l-a-county-in-expanding-homeless-services-in-skid-row#:~:text=Skid%20Row%20has%20long%20been,portion%20of%20Skid%20Row's%20population.

Vlantos, Gregory. *Socrates, Ironist and Moral Philosopher*. Ithaca, NY: Cornell University Press, 1991.

Voegelin, Eric. *Order and History, vol. III: Plato and Aristotle*. Baton Rouge: Louisiana State University Press, 1957.

———. *Plato and Aristotle*. Baton Rouge: Louisiana State University Press, 1957.

Wallnau, Lance, et al. *Invading Babylon: The 7 Mountain Mandate*. Shippensburg, PA: Destiny Image, 2013.

Walsh, Catherine E. "Introducción. Lo pedagógico y lo decolonial: Entretejiendo caminos." In *Pedagogías decoloniales: Prácticas insurgentes de resistir, (re)existir y (re)vivir*, edited by Catherine E. Walsh, 24–68. Quito: Abya-Yala, 2013.

Weingart Center. "Interim Housing." https://www.weingart.org/interim-housing#:~:text=The%20Weingart%20Shelby%20is%20a,storage%2C%20and%20pet%2Dfriendly.

Bibliography

"Weingart Center for the Homeless." Wikipedia. https://en.wikipedia.org/wiki/Weingart_Center_for_the_Homeless.

West, Cornel. *Democracy Matters: Winning the Fight against Imperialism*. New York: Penguin, 2005.

Whitehead, Andrew L., and Samuel L. Perry. *Taking America Back for God: Christian Nationalism in the United States*. New York: Oxford University Press, 2020.

Williams, David Lay. *Rousseau's Social Contract: An Introduction*. Cambridge: Cambridge University Press, 2014.

Yong, Amos. "The Bible's Story of Creation and Renewal." Sociedad Biblica Peruana, Universidad de Chiapas, Lima, Peru, July 23, 2024. Repeated and filmed via Zoom September 20, 2024. 1 hr., 22 mn., 28 sec. https://www.youtube.com/watch?v=x7UENw0_ZrY.

———. "From Every Tribe, Language, People, and Nation: Diaspora, Hybridity, and the Coming Reign of God." In *Global Diasporas and Mission*, edited by Chandler H. Im and Amos Yong. Regnum Edinburgh Centenary Series 23. Oxford: Regnum, 2014. https://www.ocms.ac.uk/wp-content/uploads/2021/01/Global_Diasporas_and_Mission.pdf.

———. *The Heteroglossic Spirit: Unruly Tongues and Translations after Pentecost*. Edited by Ekaputra Tupamahu. Eugene, OR: Cascade, forthcoming.

———. "Many Tongues, Many Biocultural Niches: A Pentecostal Missiological Response to Language Endangerment and Environmental Degradation." In *Pentecostal Missiology and Environmental Degradation*, edited by Eugene Baron and Amos Yong. Carlisle, UK: Langham Global, forthcoming.

———. *Revelation*. Belief: A Theological Commentary on the Bible. Louisville: Westminster John Knox, 2021.

Zaidman, Louise Bruit, and Pauline Schmitt Pantel. *Religion in the Ancient Greek City*. Translated by Paul Cartledge. Cambridge: Cambridge University Press, 1992.

"Zapatista School." Participedia. https://participedia.net/case/5161.

Zavis, Alexandria. "Los Angeles Skid Row Cleanup Nets Nearly 5 Tons of Refuse." *Los Angeles Times*, July 9, 2012. https://www.latimes.com/local/la-xpm-2012-jul-09-la-me-skid-row-sweep-20120710-story.html#:~:text=Hundreds%20of%20hypodermic%20needles%2C%20gallons,Friday%2C%20according%20to%20city%20officials.

Zetzel, James E. G. *Cicero and the Late Roman Republic*. Cambridge: Harvard University Press, 2017.

Zuckert, Catherine. *Plato's Philosophers: The Coherence of the Dialogues*. Chicago: University of Chicago Press, 2009.

www.ingramcontent.com/pod-product-compliance
Lightning Source LLC
Chambersburg PA
CBHW022119160426
43197CB00009B/1084